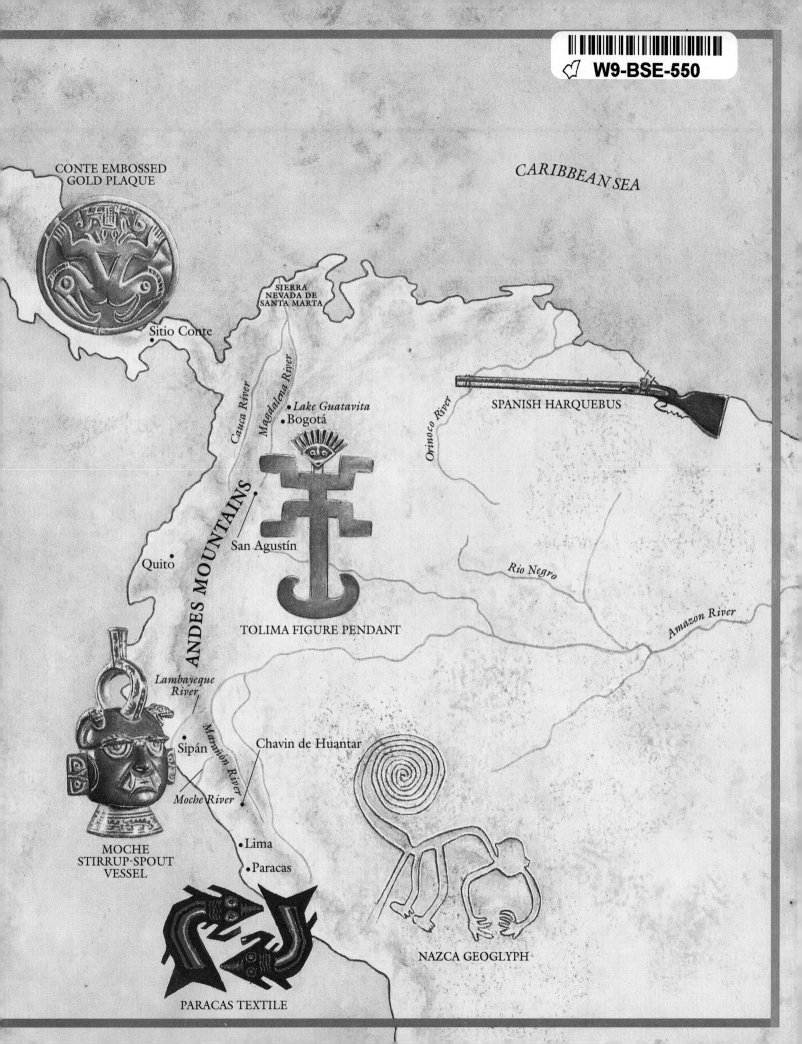

CONTE EMBOSSED
GOLD PLAQUE

CARIBBEAN SEA

SIERRA
NEVADA DE
SANTA MARTA

Sitio Conte

Cauca River

Magdalena River

Orinoco River

SPANISH HARQUEBUS

Lake Guatavita
Bogotá

San Agustín

ANDES MOUNTAINS

Quito

Rio Negro

Amazon River

TOLIMA FIGURE PENDANT

Lambayeque River

Marañón River

Sipán

Chavin de Huantar

Moche River

MOCHE
STIRRUP-SPOUT
VESSEL

Lima

Paracas

NAZCA GEOGLYPH

PARACAS TEXTILE

Other Publications:

JOURNEY THROUGH THE MIND
 AND BODY
THE WEIGHT WATCHERS® SMART
 CHOICE RECIPE COLLECTION
TRUE CRIME
THE AMERICAN INDIANS
THE ART OF WOODWORKING
ECHOES OF GLORY
THE NEW FACE OF WAR
HOW THINGS WORK
WINGS OF WAR
CREATIVE EVERYDAY COOKING
COLLECTOR'S LIBRARY OF THE
 UNKNOWN
CLASSICS OF WORLD WAR II
TIME-LIFE LIBRARY OF CURIOUS AND
 UNUSUAL FACTS
AMERICAN COUNTRY
VOYAGE THROUGH THE UNIVERSE
THE THIRD REICH
THE TIME-LIFE GARDENER'S GUIDE
MYSTERIES OF THE UNKNOWN
TIME FRAME
FIX IT YOURSELF
FITNESS, HEALTH & NUTRITION
SUCCESSFUL PARENTING
HEALTHY HOME COOKING
UNDERSTANDING COMPUTERS
LIBRARY OF NATIONS
THE ENCHANTED WORLD
THE KODAK LIBRARY OF CREATIVE
 PHOTOGRAPHY
GREAT MEALS IN MINUTES
THE CIVIL WAR
PLANET EARTH
COLLECTOR'S LIBRARY OF THE CIVIL
 WAR
THE EPIC OF FLIGHT
THE GOOD COOK
WORLD WAR II
HOME REPAIR AND IMPROVEMENT
THE OLD WEST

*For information on and a full description of
any of the Time-Life Books series listed above,
please call 1-800-621-7026 or write:*
Reader Information
Time-Life Customer Service
P.O. Box C-32068
Richmond, Virginia 23261-2068

Cover: The commanding face of a South American Moche lord evokes the rich culture of his people, who rose to greatness between AD 100 and 800 in the coastal area of northern Peru. Molded in clay, the head forms part of a bottle and is displayed against a background of a 1,000-year-old llama-wool textile. The Moche, like many other pre-Columbian peoples of South America, revered beautifully woven cloth, considering it to be more valuable than gold.

End paper: Painted by the artist Paul Breeden, the map shows the regions of Central and South America that, centuries before the Inca empire, were home to the Chavin, Moche, Paracas, Nazca, and other cultures. Their gleaming artifacts of gold fueled European adventurers' greedy quest for the precious metal. Breeden also painted the vignettes illustrating the timeline on pages 158-159.

THE SEARCH FOR
EL DORADO

Time-Life Books is a division of TIME LIFE INC.

PRESIDENT and CEO: John M. Fahey Jr.

EDITOR-IN-CHIEF: John L. Papanek

TIME-LIFE BOOKS

MANAGING EDITOR: Roberta Conlan

Executive Art Director: Ellen Robling
Director of Photography and Research: John Conrad Weiser
Senior Editors: Russell B. Adams Jr., Dale M. Brown, Janet Cave, Lee Hassig, Robert Somerville, Henry Woodhead
Director of Technology: Eileen Bradley
Director of Editorial Operations: Prudence G. Harris
Library: Louise D. Forstall

PRESIDENT: John D. Hall

Vice President, Director of Marketing: Nancy K. Jones
Vice President, New Product Development: Neil Kagan
Vice President, Book Production: Marjann Caldwell
Production Manager: Marlene Zack

Library of Congress Cataloging in Publication Data
The search for El Dorado / by the editors of Time-Life Books.
    p. cm. (Lost civilizations)
    Includes bibliographical references and index.
    ISBN 0-8094-9033-1
    1. El Dorado I. Time-Life Books. II. Series.
E121.S43 1994
9794'41—dc20   94-17846
                                                 CIP

LOST CIVILIZATIONS

SERIES EDITOR: Dale M. Brown
Administrative Editor: Philip Brandt George

Editorial staff for *The Search for El Dorado*
Art Directors: Bill McKenney, Ellen Pattisall (principals), Cindy Morgan-Jaffe, Susan K. White
Picture Editor: Charlotte Marine Fullerton
Text Editors: Charles J. Hagner (principal), Russell B. Adams Jr., Charlotte Anker
Associate Editors/Research-Writing: Robin Currie, Jacqueline L. Shaffer
Senior Copyeditors: Mary Beth Oelkers-Keegan (principal), Anne Farr
Picture Coordinator: David Herod
Editorial Assistant: Patricia D. Whiteford

Special Contributors: Donál Kevin Gordon, Donald Dale Jackson, Barbara Mallen, Valerie Moolman (text); Arlene L. Borden, Marge duMond, Ann-Louise G. Gates, Ellen Gross, Jim L. Hicks, Lydia Preston Hicks, Helen Kim, Bonnie Stutski, Elizabeth Thompson (research/writing); Roy Nanovic (index)

Correspondents: Elisabeth Kraemer-Singh (Bonn), Christine Hinze (London), Christina Lieberman (New York), Maria Vincenza Aloisi (Paris), Ann Natanson (Rome). Valuable assistance was also provided by: Tom Quinn (Bogotá), Adriana von Hagen (Lima), Judy Aspinall (London), Trini Bandrès (Madrid), Daniel Donnelly (New York), María Helena Jervis (Quito), Ann Wise (Rome).

The Consultants:
Christopher B. Donnan is director of the Fowler Museum of Cultural History at the University of California, Los Angeles. With more than 30 years of field excavating experience in Peru and some 60 books and articles to his credit, he specializes in the interpretation of Moche materials.

Jill L. McKeever Furst, professor of art history at Moore College of Art and Design in Philadelphia, has published extensively on symbolism in pre-Columbian art.

Peter T. Furst, a specialist in pre-Columbian art and ethnobotany, is adjunct professor of anthropology at the University of Pennsylvania and serves on the research staff of the University Museum.

Gordon F. McEwan is associate curator and head of the Department of New World Art at the Denver Museum. He has extensive curatorial, teaching, and field research experience in ancient Peruvian archaeology, focusing on the Valley of Cuzco and the precursors of the Inca.

Anne Paul, a research associate with the Institute of Andean Studies at the University of California, Berkeley, has published extensively on the art and architecture of the Paracas culture.

Ann Peters, a cultural anthropologist specializing in the symbolism of material culture, has concentrated her archaeological and archival research on Andean materials, specifically those of the Nazca, Paracas, and Topará cultures.

David Arthur Scott, a specialist in the study of metallurgy and the conservation of metallic artworks, is head of Museum Services of the Getty Conservation Institute based at the J. Paul Getty Museum. He is the author of many articles and a three-volume work on the use of gold, platinum, copper, and their various alloys in pre-Columbian South America.

This volume is one in a series that explores the worlds of the past, using the finds of archaeologists and other scientists to bring ancient peoples and their cultures vividly to life.

Other volumes in the series include:

THE SEARCH FOR EL DORADO

By the Editors of Time-Life Books

TIME-LIFE BOOKS, ALEXANDRIA, VIRGINIA

CONTENTS

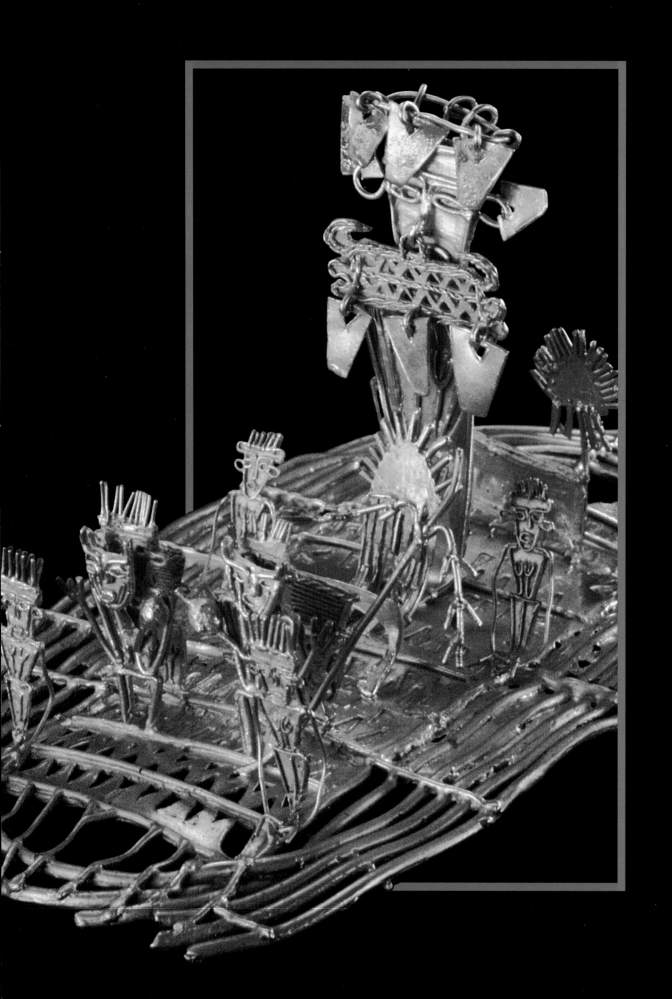

THE GOLDEN ENCHANTMENT OF SOUTH AMERICA

It looks rather unspectacular, this quiet lake in the 8,000-foot-high altiplano 30 miles northeast of Bogotá, Colombia—but how should a dream vision look? How can a single place or picture encapsulate the romance of the eternal quest, the buoyant hope and dogged faith that forever fall short of realization? For this neatly circular, smooth-surfaced, and forest-fringed mountain tarn has a legend and history like none other: It is Lake Guatavita, the place of the Golden Man—the seat of El Dorado.

It was here, legends said, that offerings of gold and emeralds were made when the Indian ruler the Spaniards called El Dorado sprinkled gold dust on his skin *(page 11)* and dove into the cold water to appease his god. The El Dorado tale seized the imagination of the conquistadors and set them plodding over mountains and through jungles for a century and more, ruthlessly disrupting entire cultures as they pursued a prize that seemed always just a few days' march farther on. El Dorado, one of the world's most enchanting and enduring legends, also came to be one of the cruelest and costliest, in terms of lives, money, and the eradication of native peoples.

When the treasure seekers finally identified 130-foot-deep Guatavita *(pages 8-9)* as the lake in the El Dorado legend, they attacked it with all the tools and ingenuity at their command. In the 16th century thousands of shovel-wielding Indian slaves hacked a

Wearing an elaborate nosepiece and headdress, a seated Muisca king flanked by his courtiers rides an eight-inch-long gold raft in a scene that reflects the ancient legend of El Dorado, the Golden Man.

canyon out of the shoreline in an attempt to drain the lake, while in later centuries entrepreneurs dug tunnels with drills and steel-clawed machines. And, almost always, they found gold—not all that they hoped for, but enough to keep them coming back. For that was the most intriguing fact of all about El Dorado: The gold was real, and it was there.

The precious metal had helped drive the exploration of the New World from the beginning. Europeans searched for gold in the tropics—first along Africa's Gold Coast, then in the Western Hemisphere—because they associated its color with the sun, and because they believed it "grew" better there. Columbus had sought gold throughout the West Indies, and found it on the island of Hispaniola, which briefly served as his base in the New World in 1493. The subsequent discoveries of Aztec and Inca treasures by Hernán Cortés and Francisco Pizarro had thrilled and beckoned a generation of adventurers in Spain and throughout Europe. By the time latecomers first heard the El Dorado story, probably in 1541, expeditions led by Spaniards and the German banking house of Welser had been pushing into the South American interior from the Andean realm of the conquered Incas and from the Atlantic and Caribbean coasts for a decade. (The Holy Roman Emperor Charles V, who was also king of Spain, had granted Welser the province of Venezuela as collateral for a loan.)

In the ensuing century the gold-smitten Europeans made one doomed trek after another, across an unforgiving landscape where a dozen dangers—jaguars and crocodile-like caimans, cannibals and poisoned arrows, thirst and starvation and tropical diseases—awaited them. One by one they set forth with their banners and giddy hopes,

Surrounded by green Andean hills, Lake Guatavita still displays the trench (left) *made by Antonio de Sepúlveda's attempt in the 1580s to drain the body of water and find its treasures. Guatavita was one of five lakes sacred to the Muisca, each the supposed dwelling place of a deity who required offerings of emeralds and gold.*

only to return two or three years later in defeat and tatters, their numbers halved or worse. A splinter band from one company floated nearly the 4,000-mile length of the Amazon. In another expedition a group of rebels killed their leaders and cut a bloody swath halfway across the continent. At the end of the 16th century the English buccaneer Sir Walter Raleigh turned up in South America on the same greedy quest, which in the end cost him his reputation and his head.

With the passing of the era of the conquistadors, the hunt for gold in Central and South America subsided to sporadic spasms that persisted into the 20th century. In the meantime another quest began, driven by a desire not for treasure but for knowledge—not only of those civilizations all but obliterated by the gold seekers, but also of the magnificent societies that flowered and disappeared long before the conquistadors arrived. Scientists trying to understand these lost cultures start their study with the gold that lured the invaders—fine jewelry, ornaments, fishing hooks, sewing utensils, and other items made from the precious metal.

Such gold pieces, along with early Spanish chronicles, rare pottery and textiles, and scattered ruins, remain the primary sources for what is known about the dozens of civilizations that once flourished in South America before the Inca empire. And the artifacts themselves often come from graverobbers known as *huaqueros*, whose looting of burial sites constituted a second wave of destruction and whose information on the details of their finds has proved unreliable at best. In recent years, political and drug-related violence has added yet another obstacle to archaeology in the region. As a result, scholars' understanding of such pre-Inca cultures as the Chavin, Moche, Paracas, Nazca, and others reaching back as far as 2,800 years remains incomplete. Despite some thrilling recent finds along Peru's north coast, on the arid Paracas Peninsula to the south, and elsewhere, these peoples, who like the great Incas lacked writing, remain mysterious and all but nameless, identified only by the areas where they happened to live. And yet, paradoxically, their grave goods—and even their mummified remains—have increasingly enabled archaeologists to reconstruct numerous aspects of their daily lives and rituals.

The El Dorado legend, which loomed so large in the chain of events that brought havoc to the Indians and their culture, first appeared in print in the work of the chronicler Gonzalo Fernández de Oviedo in 1541, three years after the conquistador Gonzalo Jiménez de Quesada *(page 19)* had conquered the area between Bogotá and the north coast of South America. The Indian groups living in and around New Granada, as Quesada christened the region, were such accomplished and prolific goldworkers that the Europeans laid claim to an enormous booty. The one-fifth share reserved for Charles V alone came to more than 385 pounds of fine, or 22-carat, gold (making the total of fine gold taken approximately 2,000 pounds) and a large quantity of base, or 14-carat, gold and *tumbaga*, an alloy of gold and copper. Each soldier received five pounds of fine gold and nine ounces of base gold. News of Quesada's windfall no doubt sparked the interest of Oviedo, who lived on Hispaniola. Then he heard Spaniards who had been in the recently conquered Inca city of Quito, 450 miles southwest of Bogotá, tell of yet another source of gold, which they learned of from Indians.

Oviedo wrote of a "great lord or prince" who covered his naked body daily with "gold dust as fine as ground salt." The leader scorned the gold armor worn by other lords because "to powder oneself with gold is exotic and more costly, for he washes away at night what he puts on each morning."

This initial version contains no mention of a lake, but a letter written a year later by soldier-historian Pedro de Cieza de León identified a "Lake El Dorado" in a populous land east of Quito. Subsequent refinements, in both prose and poetry, appeared in the late 16th and 17th centuries, culminating in the tale of El Dorado's ritual dip in Lake Guatavita, told most engagingly by a Spanish priest named Pedro Simón. "There is a lake in the land of this chief onto which, placed in the middle of a well-made raft, he went a few times a year," Pedro Simón wrote in the 1620s, repeating some details and adding new ones. "He went naked but his body was covered from head to hands and feet with a kind of sticky turpentine on which much fine gold dust was scattered. In the morning sun of a clear day he would go to the middle of the lake and make offerings by throwing emeralds and pieces of gold into the water while he pronounced certain words. Then, washing his body with herbs like soap, the gold on his skin fell into the water and the ceremony ended." Pedro Simón added that other lords joined the chief in throwing valuables into the lake. An account published a decade later embellished the tale still more by including a ceremonial chorus of trumpets and flutes as well as smoky braziers on shore. This version also connected the ritual to the accession of a new ruler.

Time and imagination further gilded the legend until the lake was transformed into a city of gold, then an entire province where all the drinking vessels were golden and every living thing in the realm—every bird, fish, tree, and vine—was said to have its counterpart in the precious metal. By the time Sir Walter Raleigh arrived in 1595 at Port of Spain, Trinidad, with five ships, El Dorado had evolved into a gold-rich kingdom known as Manoa, an Indian name for lake. The realm supposedly stood on the shores of a body of water in present-day Venezuela, south of the Orinoco River. One explanation of the metamorphosis of El Dorado from individual to lake to city has the legend deriving from Indian tales of the great Inca capital of Cuzco, almost 1,000 miles southeast of Quito, where the Temple of the Sun was described by Cieza de León as one of "the richest in gold and silver to be found anywhere in the world." Another version holds that the golden city was the headquarters of the Inca chief Manco Capac, who escaped the Spaniards and fled with his followers and treasure to the forested fastness of their final redoubt, Vilcabamba.

The first explorer to sally forth with the specific goal of finding El Dorado was Gonzalo Pizarro, brother of the conqueror of the

While tribesmen carouse in the background, one attendant covers a naked chieftain with resin and another puffs gold dust on his body in this 1590 depiction of the El Dorado ceremony by Flemish artist Théodore de Bry. Although the rite seems to have ended about 100 years before the engraving appeared, reports of the Golden Man and the treasures tossed into sacrificial waters by the Indians continued to draw conquistadors into the region.

Incas, Francisco Pizarro, and a man who had already earned a reputation for cruelty to Indians. Gonzalo Pizarro outfitted a 220-man brigade with weapons, horses, llamas, and pigs for meat and headed east from Quito in February 1541. Accompanied by 4,000 shackled Indian porters, he struggled across the Andes before plunging into the jungle, where his soldiers had to slash a trail with machetes. Pizarro asked the Indians he met for the location of the rich country he had heard about; when their answers failed to satisfy him, he burned them to death or threw them to hunting dogs specially trained to attack Indians.

The adventurers slogged on for several months, bedeviled by heavy rains, losing many of their supplies in a flash flood, the Indian porters dying or escaping until most were gone. When Pizarro reached a broad river, probably the Napo River, a tributary of the Amazon, he ordered a sizable boat built. Wood was plentiful, but the explorers had to take the metal they required from the shoes of the dead horses. With some men aboard and the rest trying to keep pace ashore, they labored downstream for 43 days before halting, their food stores exhausted. Then the expedition divided, Pizarro and one group remaining in place while his deputy Francisco de Orellana and 60 men continued downstream in the boat to find food.

But Orellana was unable to sail back upstream against the strong current, a failure Pizarro later attributed to treachery. Orellana and his men instead made the first known passage of the world's greatest river, down the Napo River to the Amazon and all the way to the Atlantic, the journey consuming about five months. The Indians they encountered reacted in different ways, some fleeing in terror, others providing food, still others attacking with clubs and spears. The most accomplished people the voyagers met were the Omagua, who impressed Orellana with their roads, storage tanks filled with turtles, an ample food supply, and the large ceramic jars they crafted. But the Spaniards, as they were to do repeatedly, soon wore out their welcome and provoked a battle by stealing food.

Below the river's junction with the south-flowing Rio Negro, Orellana's men skirmished with an even more surprising tribe. According to an account written by Friar Gaspar de Carvajal, who traveled with Orellana, these Indians were led by 10 or 12 "female captains." The women "fought so courageously," Carvajal wrote, "that the men did not dare turn their backs. [They were] very white and tall, with long braided hair wound about their heads. They are very

THE GEOGRAPHY AND GEOLOGY OF GOLD

The gold that sparked the quest for El Dorado originated as a result of violent activity within the earth. More than 100 million years ago the South American continental plate, one of the sections that make up the planet's crust, slammed into the Nazca plate, which lies below the Pacific Ocean. The impact crumpled the continent's western edge, forming the mountain system known as the Andes. As part of the heavier Nazca plate slid beneath the South American plate, much of it melted. Superheated magma rose and was intruded into the newly forming mountains above. As the magma cooled, gold and other minerals crystallized in the rock.

Over time some of the gold weathered out and settled in streams and rivers, forming deposits called placers. Placer gold, ranging in size from dust to nuggets *(below)*, was a major source of the metal for early gold cultures. Not only did the Indians come to pan for it in rivers, but they also dug placer mines in relict stream and river deposits.

The Tairona and the Muis-ca, in what is now Colombia, and goldworking groups along the Peruvian coast lacked their own gold, and thus had to trade with people who had access to it in the Andes. The map shows areas in Central and South America where various gold cultures flourished between 1000 BC and AD 1500.

robust, [carry] bows and arrows, and do as much fighting as ten Indian men." Such a foe, the Spaniards were quick to conclude, could only be Amazons, the mythical tribe of women that Columbus, Cortés, and other explorers believed ruled the dark jungles of the New World and by whose name its greatest river is known today.

Amazingly, Orellana and most of his men reached the Atlantic safely and sailed northwest along the northeast coast of South America to Margarita, a small Spanish-held island where they turned up in September 1542. Pizarro had meanwhile been reduced to eating horses and dogs and even saddle leather before his return to Quito with fewer than 100 men three months earlier. On their arrival, a witness wrote, Pizarro's scarred and nearly naked men kissed the ground in gratitude. Famished, many could "eat but little at a time till their stomachs became accustomed to digest their food."

Two other expeditions departed from jumping-off points in northwestern South America the year that Pizarro left Quito. The first, led by Hernán Pérez de Quesada, set out with 260 men from the territory of the peaceful and accomplished Muisca people in the Bogotá area, discovered only a few years previously by Pérez's brother Gonzalo Jiménez de Quesada. Philipp von Hutten, the nephew of the German humanist Ulrich von Hutten, commanded the second. Sent to conquer Venezuela on behalf of the Welsers, von Hutten started from the Caribbean coast in the company of 130 men.

Pérez de Quesada's band, which included 6,000 captive Indian porters, marched south along the east side of the Andean cordillera in search of a tribe called the Waipis, who were said to know El Dorado. Food began to run short in the outer Amazon Basin, where the expedition's chronicler reported that Quesada and his men journeyed several days with no sustenance save roots. The many rivers that crisscrossed the area further weakened the explorers, as they had to build dozens of bridges. "Some soldiers and the majority of the Indian porters died," the reporter noted matter-of-factly.

As the terrain became more manageable, the Indians Quesada encountered grew ever more aggressive. He turned west toward the mountains just north of the border of present-day Ecuador, near the headwaters of the Caquetá River, after hearing "good reports" about the country from Indians who doubtless wanted only to be rid of him. But when he reached the foothills one tribe seized five of his

One Indian digs for gold alongside a jungle river while two others sift the gravel with shallow wooden pans, called bateas, *in this 16th-century woodcut. "They take the earth, little by little, from the mine to the washing place," wrote the Spanish chronicler Gonzalo Fernández de Oviedo, "and there they clean it with water to see if there is gold in the* bateas."

14

men and sliced them into quarters in full view of the rest. This struck Quesada as perversely encouraging—could these warriors be guarding the approach to El Dorado?—but disillusionment followed: The adventurers entered a valley they recognized as territory already occupied by the Spaniards, part of the well-traveled road between Quito and the lands of the Muisca, also known as the Chibcha. Having lost 80 soldiers and several thousand Indians, the remnants of Quesada's dispirited company trudged wearily back to Bogotá.

Von Hutten, a veteran of earlier German-Spanish expeditions, covered more ground than Quesada—his men hiked almost the entire length of Colombia. For part of the way, on the east slope of the Andes, they took the same route, after von Hutten's men found and followed Quesada's tracks. Before long von Hutten too ran out of provisions, and the chronicler Fernández de Oviedo wrote that they were forced to live on corn and ants. Skin diseases beset them, "pestiferous tumors and poisonous ulcers," transforming the journey into what Oviedo called a "theater of miseries."

The German tried a new tack when he heard of a place called Guagua, or Omagua—apparently a different Omagua from the one Orellana had found on the Amazon. The Omagua people were said to be "very rich" with "enormous towns" in their homeland along

the Guaviare River in central Colombia. When the troops reached what they thought was Omagua land, von Hutten beheld in the distance a "town of disproportionate size . . . compact and well-ordered" with a large house or temple in the center. These Indians, they were told, possessed a life-size golden effigy of a goddess.

Certain that this was at last the promised land, von Hutten and another officer tried to capture two Omagua, only to be repelled when the Indians wounded them both with lances that pierced their bodies below their armor. Von Hutten, with just 40 men against a now-aroused Indian force of several thousand, decided to go back to Venezuela for more men, but he would not get the chance. On his return he was ensnared in a political struggle between Germans and Spaniards, seized by his enemies, and decapitated in a notably grisly way—with a blunt machete.

The people of Spain seemed to be of two minds about the pursuit of treasure in the territory they called the Spanish Main. One part of the population, ready to believe that almost anything was possible in the New World after the extraordinary discoveries in Mexico and Peru, burned with gold fever. This group was "so desirous of novelties," recalled one English chronicler, "that what way soever they bee called with a becke only or soft whispering voyce . . . they speedily prepare themselves to flie and forsake certainties." Oviedo wrote of one expedition, "I do not believe that any of those who took part would have taken so much trouble to get into Paradise."

But other Spaniards protested on moral grounds against colonialism and the Europeans' appalling cruelty to the Indians—and were for a time strikingly successful. Led by a bishop from Mexico named Bartolomé de las Casas, the reformers persuaded Charles V to issue a set of liberal pro-Indian laws in 1542. The statutes so outraged the conquistadors in Peru that they rose in open rebellion against the mother country and drafted Gonzalo Pizarro to lead them. For four years he ruled as dictator of the colony. But even after the crown revoked most of the laws and Pizarro was captured and hanged outside Cuzco in 1548 by an administrator sent from Spain to subdue the rebels, the issue still stood unresolved.

A great debate was held in 1550 to give a thorough hearing to both sides. Las Casas argued that the unchris-

NEW WORLD MEDICAL MYSTERY

Scientists have long assumed that the great dying off that occurred among the Indians of the Americas after the arrival of the Europeans was caused in large measure by the diseases brought by the invaders—tuberculosis among them—against which the Indians had little, if any, resistance. But recent studies carried out on a thousand-year-old mummy of a woman from southern Peru have helped modify that view, at least as far as tuberculosis is concerned.

When pathologist Arthur Aufderheide of the University of Minnesota autopsied the poorly preserved body *(below)*, he found a lump on one lung

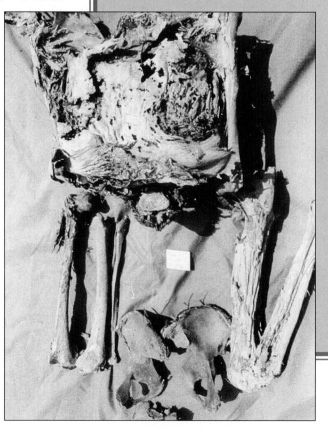

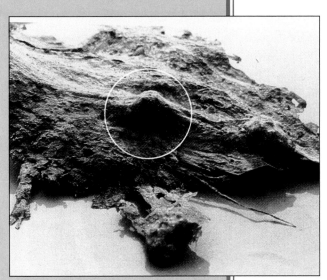

(circled area, above) and two more on lymph nodes, indicative of the presence of the disease. Using a new technique of DNA analysis called polymerase chain reaction, Aufderheide and a biochemist colleague at the university were able to clone billions of copies of the mummy's genetic material. Their study revealed a fragment of DNA found only in TB bacteria, confirming that their diagnosis was correct.

The woman had lived to be 40 or 45, a ripe old age in those days—and TB was not the cause of her death. But the fact that she had the disease shows that it was indeed present in the Americas before the Europeans brought their own contagions to the new land. How then did tuberculosis get there? Did migrants bring it from Asia via the Bering land bridge many thousands of years ago? The questions await answers.

tian outrages committed in the king's name endangered the monarch's soul. His main opponent contended that the superiority of Spanish civilization and religion legitimized the conquests. Though inconclusive, the debate prompted Charles V to take the remarkable step of baning all expeditions and exploration. The resulting suspension of journeys of conquest—and the welcome respite it offered the Indians—persisted through most of the decade of the 1550s.

When the ban was lifted in 1559 it was instantly clear that gold mania among the New World Spaniards had not abated in the slightest. New rumors reached Peru that appeared to corroborate Francisco de Orellana's story of the rich Omagua tribe on the Amazon River, and gold seekers were soon hurrying to enlist in a new trek commanded by Pedro de Ursúa, an officer renowned for his success in quelling Indian uprisings. Ursúa recruited a motley band of disaffected veterans and malcontents, the kind of men the Spanish novelist Miguel de Cervantes had in mind when he wrote of the Indies as a "refuge for Spain's despairing, shrine of the mutineer, [and] asylum for the murderer." Ursúa, enjoined to conquer the province of "Omagua an Dorado," set sail in a fleet of small boats on an Amazon tributary in September 1560. With him were 370 Spaniards, several thousand captive Indians, and his handsome and plucky mistress, doña Inéz de Atienza.

The expedition deteriorated almost immediately. The men muttered mutinously under Ursúa's orders that they build a settlement along the Amazon during the rainy season, which soon descended upon them. They killed what Indians they met and ran short of food. On New Year's Day 1561 Ursúa's men murdered him in his hammock and installed another officer as a figurehead commander. The real leader, a vicious ex-soldier named Lope de Aguirre, seethed with a desire not to find El Dorado but to return to Peru at the head of a rebel army. Aguirre persuaded the titular leader, Fernando de Guzmán, to proclaim himself "prince" of Peru, but within a few months he grew impatient with Guzmán too and ordered the execution of both the prince and Inéz. The killers plunged a sword through Guzmán; Inéz was stabbed more than 20 times.

As the party sailed down the Amazon in two large boats, Aguirre systematically killed anyone he suspected of dissent, especially "persons of quality," nearly halving his expedition's size. Avoiding the Omagua lands, Aguirre finally reached the Atlantic in July 1561 and sailed to the isle of Margarita, where his band murdered the governor and seized control, then set off overland for the triumphant return to Peru. But Aguirre's luck ran out when his men began deserting and an army marched from Peru to defeat him. In the Venezuelan town of Barquisimeto, 170 miles west of present-day Caracas, he authored a final barbarity—the murder of his own 16-year-old daughter, ostensibly to save her from the onrushing royal troops. Aguirre's men slew him with their long guns, quartered his body, and displayed the sections at the town gates as a warning to other potential rebels.

But though Aguirre and Ursúa were now dead, along with Philipp von Hutten and Gonzalo Pizarro, the El Dorado dream still lived. Another expedition in 1566, regrettably without a chronicler, covered more than a thousand hard miles in Peru and Colombia, establishing that El Dorado lay neither in the Omagua lands nor in the country immediately east of Quito. The focus now shifted farther east, to the flat grasslands called llanos that stretch between the Andes and the Orinoco basin. And this time temptation seized one of the great veterans of New World exploration, the discoverer and governor of New Granada, Gonzalo Jiménez de Quesada.

After receiving the governorship of a newly designated province on the llanos, Quesada, who was in his late sixties, left Bogotá with 300 soldiers, 1,500 Indians, and large herds of horses and cattle in December 1569 to found new towns and locate El Dorado. For several months they plodded through a country that was alternately dust-dry, swampy, and swept by heavy rains. Many died from disease and hunger; others deserted. Quesada at first hanged captured deserters, then let those who wanted to leave do so. Doggedly he pushed onward for two and a half years, but the result was another long list of dead: 250 Spaniards and all but 30 of the Indians. A report from the survivors who reached Bogotá coldly summarized his disaster: "He has made no settlement and achieved nothing."

The husband of Quesada's niece, Antonio de Berrio, had already spent a lifetime soldiering for Spain when he learned that Quesada had selected him to continue the pursuit of El Dorado. The old conquistador, who died of leprosy in 1579, bequeathed both his governorship and his estates to the 59-year-old Berrio, who proved to be an inspired choice. Courageous and indefatigable, Berrio became the most ardent and committed seeker of the Golden Man yet seen, while his life, in the end, became a metaphor for the wretched futility of the quest.

Berrio was persuaded early, primarily by the accounts of Indians, that the land of gold lay not in the llanos as Jiménez de Quesada had believed but in the forested mountains south of the middle Orinoco River, in what is now southern Venezuela. On his first, 17-month-long expedition, begun in 1583, he withstood an attack by Achagua Indians and heard stories from his captives of a "very large laguna," called Manoa, high among the peaks, on the far side of which were "great settlements and a very great number of people, and great riches of gold and precious stones." The lake, with its evocation of the body of water in the El Dorado legend, was said to be so large that it took three days to paddle across it *(page 23)*.

When he reached the Orinoco and saw the mountains beyond, Berrio was certain, as he later wrote to King Charles's successor to the throne of Spain, Philip II, that he had found "the cordillera so ardently desired and sought for 70 years past, and which has cost the lives of so many Spaniards." But when he prepared to probe the canyons and foothills on the trail to Manoa, he could muster only 13 fit men from his original force of 100. They climbed within six miles of the summit in search of the lake before the steepness and his men's weakness persuaded him to halt and return to Bogotá. He lost only eight men, a negligible number by the standards of the Spanish Main and evidence of his skills as a commander.

Berrio's second try, in 1587, with 97 men, six canoes, and abundant supplies, met with no greater success. Again he crossed the Orinoco and tried repeatedly to reach the high peaks, but again he came up short, despite hiking the lower slopes for some 600 miles. Hostile Indians and malaria beleaguered the men, and the 68-year-old commander himself fell ill. A mutinous officer delivered the final blow, absconding with most of the men and all the canoes. Enraged, Berrio had to decamp and march back to Bogotá.

Founder of Bogotá, capital of the modern-day republic of Colombia, Gonzalo Jiménez de Quesada led the largest Spanish expedition into Muisca territory and was the first European to reach Guatavita. To the Indians, the bearded strangers looked like gods, and to appease them the Muisca left young children as sacrifices in the path of the invaders.

PERCY FAWCETT AND JIMMIE ANGEL: MEN IN THE GRIP OF A PASSION

Since the earliest mention of the existence of a gold-filled sacred lake somewhere in South America, the pull of El Dorado has been strong. For some, the lure has been the age-old lust for gold; for others, it has been the fantasy of a vanished civilization awaiting discovery.

Colonel Percy Harrison Fawcett was convinced that a lost city lay deep in the Mato Grosso jungles of Brazil. After years of research, the former military engineer was sure he could find the site—which he dubbed "Z"—and in 1925 the 58-year-old Briton set off into the unknown with his son Jack and his son's 18-year-old companion, Raleigh Rimell. They were not heard from, and people began to worry about their safety.

Three years later a search party sent out to find the men returned empty-handed. However, in 1932 a Swiss trapper claimed that he had seen Fawcett living with an Indian tribe; when the trapper returned to the forests to rescue him, he too vanished. Since then, there have been various reported sightings of an elderly white man in the Mato Grosso and of fair, blue-eyed Indians, reputedly the offspring of the younger Fawcett and his friend. But none of these claims have been substantiated, and it seems most

likely that the three explorers met an unhappy end at the hands of hostile Indians.

A year before Fawcett's trek into the Brazilian interior, American aviator Jimmie Angel was drawn into his own quest. In 1924 an aged prospector paid the 25-year-old pilot $5,000—in gold—to fly him to a secret location in the mostly unexplored jungles of eastern Venezuela. The oldster directed Angel by a meandering and perhaps deliberately misleading course to the top of a 9,000-foot-high mesa-like mountain. There, according to Angel, the two men spent three days happily plucking gold nuggets from a stream and stuffing them into gunnysacks before

a storm forced them to make a hasty departure. Unfortunately for Angel, only his companion knew precisely where they were, and when the old man died several years later, he took the secret with him to the grave.

The search for the mountaintop became an obsession that would fill Angel's remaining years. In 1935 he moved to Venezuela, took a job with a mining company, and spent his spare time exploring. Although he became the first white man to behold the world's highest waterfall, at 3,212 feet, which was later named for him, he spied no sign of the golden peak. Discouraged, Angel eventually moved to California, but he refused to give up. He was 57 when he set off on his last attempt to find the lost mountain, in 1956. A cross wind flipped his small Cessna while he taxied on a runway in Panama, and he died soon afterward of a cerebral hemorrhage. His ashes were scattered over Angel Falls.

Some of the single-mindedness of Percy Fawcett is evident in this 1911 photograph of the English adventurer, who disappeared into the Brazilian forests in 1925 after assuring his wife, "You need have no fear of any failure." Colonel Fawcett's search for a legendary city in the South American jungle was the inspiration for Sir Arthur Conan Doyle's tale of adventure Lost World.

Water plunges over the spectacular Angel Falls, the great cataract named for Jimmie Angel (inset), the plucky American bush pilot who came upon it in 1935.

Flying from the top of the falls toward the jungle below, Angel estimated with his plane's altimeter that the drop was more than 3,000 feet.

But the old campaigner still refused to give up. In 1590 he set off again, this time leading 70 Spaniards, along with Indian supporters, equipped with everything from harquebuses to wine. He sought a pass through the cordillera farther down the Orinoco, but unscalable peaks blocked his progress once again. The food ran out, and disease drove the starving men mad, resulting in the deaths of 30 Spaniards and 200 Indians. Berrio, however, decided not to turn back. Suspecting that the remaining troops were thinking of deserting, he ordered the horses killed, thereby precluding flight on horseback while providing a fresh meat supply. The party then sailed several hundred miles east to the Orinoco's confluence with the Caroní River, which flows out of the highlands that straddle Brazil's present-day border with Guyana, Surinam, and French Guiana. Here at last, Berrio thought, was the gateway to El Dorado. Beyond an upstream waterfall that rendered the Caroní unnavigable, he was convinced, lay Manoa and "the greatest grandeur and wealth that the world holds."

He needed assistance desperately. More men had died, and a parasite-caused disease had blinded others. When a plea for reinforcements from the island of Margarita went unheeded, Berrio himself sailed down the Orinoco delta to Trinidad and then on to Margarita to seek help. His most valuable recruit turned out to be a talented promoter and true believer named Domingo de Vera, who enlisted enough men in Caracas to lead a short foray up the Caroní. On his return Vera reported confidently that no fewer than two million people lived in the highlands, that they habitually wore every variety of gold ornament, and that Manoa itself lay only 11 days' march beyond the farthest point he had reached. Berrio meanwhile embraced a new but erroneous notion to explain the presence of this still unseen land of plenty: Manoa was where the Incas originated; they had gone from there to conquer Peru.

The wizened soldier, now 74 years old, was running out of time. Political rivals refused to help him recruit men and money for a new expedition. Back in New Granada, his wife, Quesada's niece, died. In desperation he sent Vera to Spain to see if he could convert his El Dorado stories into tangible support. But before Vera could return, a new player in the El Dorado drama appeared onstage, a man who could change everything: Sir Walter Raleigh.

Raleigh, at 41, had already enjoyed a brilliant career—gallant courtier to Queen Elizabeth I, poet, pirate, and sea captain, colonizer of Virginia—but a secret marriage to one of the queen's attendants

Efsekebe F.

MANOA odel DORADO

LACVS SALSVS PARIME.

A 16th-century engraving locates the mythical city of El Dorado, or Manoa, on the edge of a rumored inland salt lake called Parima, and goes so far as to show Indian porters transferring boats and supplies overland to the lake from the headwaters of a nearby river. One French cartographer included Manoa and Parima on a map published as late as 1806.

had stained his reputation, and at the moment he was in ill favor. Thinking a coup in the New World, perhaps the conquest of the golden kingdom the Spaniards called El Dorado, could restore his previous luster, he turned up off Trinidad in 1595.

Raleigh knew about Vera's trip up the Caroní River and Berrio's expeditions, probably because an English captain had seized a Spanish ship carrying a report from Vera. He requested a meeting with Berrio to learn more about El Dorado, but when Berrio spurned his invitation—relations between England and Spain were chronically strained—Raleigh attacked his base on Trinidad and captured Berrio. Subjected to a courtly interrogation, the old war-horse tried to mislead and discourage the Englishman, but Raleigh, undeceived, ordered his men to build small boats for a month-long voyage up the Orinoco delta to the edge of the promised land.

The hot, uncomfortable passage through the tortuous delta was a revelation for Raleigh. "There was never any prison in England," he wrote in his Elizabethan style, "that coulde be founde more unsavory and lothsome, especially to my selfe." When he and his

23

band emerged onto the main river, he courteously questioned several Indians *(page 25)* and heard enough to confirm his notion that El Dorado lay farther up the Caroní. He also learned about a nearby gold mine, and his men gathered a load of promising rocks to take back. Then, since Raleigh intended this only as a reconnaissance trip, he returned to the coast, released Berrio, and sailed home.

Interesting the queen in conquering Guiana—as the region bounded by the Atlantic and the Orinoco, Negro, and Amazon Rivers was then known—posed his most daunting challenge; Elizabeth professed no interest whatever. Raleigh wrote a book, *The Discoverie of the Large, Rich and Bewtiful Empire of Guiana, with a relation of the Great and Golden City of Manoa (which the Spaniards call El Dorado),* that repeated and blended the most tantalizing El Dorado stories. In Raleigh's version, not just the Golden Man but all the resident Indians anointed themselves with powdered gold. In Guiana, he penned, stood "more rich and bewtifull cities, more temples adorned with golden images" than in either Mexico or Peru.

When Elizabeth remained unmoved by his prose, Raleigh dispatched lieutenants on further reconnaissance trips while he worked his way back into the queen's favor by sailing in several campaigns against the Spaniards. All this came to naught, however, when his enemy James VI of Scotland, who favored friendly relations with Spain, succeeded Elizabeth in 1603. Implicated in a probably trumped-up plot to supplant the new king, Raleigh was convicted of treason, sentenced to death, and imprisoned in the Tower of London, where he languished for 12 years.

Berrio meanwhile played out the tag ends of his long quest. His deputy, Domingo de Vera, successfully recruited some 2,000 eager argonauts in Spain in 1596. But a shortage of food and persistent attacks by the formidable Caribs—a group related to the Indians after whom the Caribbean Sea was named—quickly reduced this unwieldy band. Berrio, moving up the Orinoco to the mouth of the Caroní but too old to go farther, mounted one final expedition up the Caroní valley under another lieutenant. This group disintegrated when its leader died and the Indians wiped out the demoralized remnants. Berrio, truest of the true believers, went to his God in 1597.

Raleigh, however, wasn't done yet. Released on probation in 1616, the 64-year-old corsair was allowed to organize an expedition of 13 ships and a thousand men to chase his fantasy one more time, on condition that he make no hostile moves against the Spaniards.

A local chief welcomes Sir Walter Raleigh's party to Guiana in 1595, treating his guests to a meal of venison, peccary, jungle fowl, and parakeets and providing Raleigh with his first taste of pineapple. The opportunistic Englishman—who had traveled with his men up the Orinoco in rowboats rather than the oceangoing vessel shown in the background—intended to find the city of gold and make his queen, Elizabeth I, empress of El Dorado.

But when he sent his men up the Orinoco delta while he remained back on the ship, they promptly overran a Spanish village. Their few tepid attempts to find the rumored gold mine proved fruitless as always. When Raleigh learned of the attack, he knew that he was now in effect a fugitive. Rejecting the idea of fleeing, he sailed back to England in 1618 to face his accusers, but this time he was sentenced to death by the ax. Gallant and graceful to the last, he felt the executioner's weapon and remarked that it would "cure all sorrows," then commanded the hesitant axman to strike.

Guatavita, the mysterious cup-shaped lake in the Spanish-occupied Muisca Indian land near Bogotá, had been identified early as a possible site of El Dorado but remained largely neglected during the years of hot-eyed quest and persistent futility. In the 1550s the chronicler Cieza de León wrote of a lake near Bogotá that, if drained, would yield a "quantity of gold and emeralds that the Indians threw

TREASURE TO RIVAL THE GOLD OF TROY

Heavy flooding in 1927 caused the Río Grande de Coclé in Panama to change course and cut through a pre-Columbian grave-yard, washing a wealth of riches into the open. Soon gold objects began appearing in Panama City, where representatives of Harvard University's Peabody Museum purchased many of them. Tracing the gold to its source, they entered into an agreement with the Conte family, who owned the site, to allow scientific excavations to begin. Not only did the site promise riches; it was that rarest of things—a pristine burial ground, unplundered by either Spaniards or huaqueros.

During the dry seasons of 1930, 1931, and 1933, the diggers uncovered no fewer than 59 graves. Among these was Grave 26, the largest and wealthiest, containing 22 skeletons and hundreds of potsherds and gold objects. The finds so closely paralleled the early Spanish descriptions of Indian burial practices that the investigators dated the graveyard to AD 1300-1500. (Years later, stylistic comparisons and carbon-14 dating would prove the site to be much older—AD 450-900.)

So much material was uncovered in those three seasons that the decision was made to concentrate on assessing the discoveries and writing up detailed reports about the items rather than doing further exploring. While the Peabody may have given up, the owners did not. Through the Harvard archaeologists, they contacted the University Museum in Philadelphia.

In 1940 the onset of World War II shut down digs in the Old World, and money became available in the New. The Philadelphia team expanded on the previous work—and soon hit pay dirt. In the last grave to be explored, Burial 11, the excavators uncovered three levels yielding 23 interments and thousands of pieces of pottery and gold. "By both quantity and quality," the team's leader wrote later, "this 'find' was one of the richest, if not the richest, ever made in America by a scientific expedition from the United States."

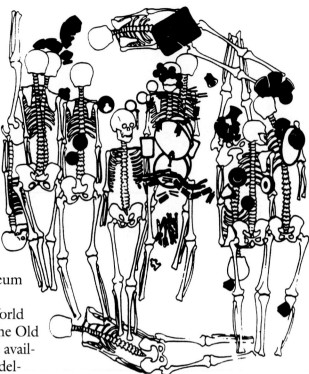

One of several diagrams made of the three levels making up Burial 11 shows skeletons and grave goods jammed together. "With due exaggeration," the chief archaeologist wrote, "the gold aglittering in this grave makes Schliemann's treasure of—was it Agamemnon?—and that of Ecuador look like pikers. Every time we take up another potsherd or knife out another piece of dirt there's another gold ornament. Give it a wipe or a little scrape with a stick and it's as beautiful as it ever was or ever will be."

Golden pendants like these two, attesting to the talents of Panamanian goldsmiths, lay on or near the skeleton of a chief in Burial 11. The nearly five-inch-long, reptilian-eyed jaguar at left was cast by the lost-wax method and then set with an emerald, which was probably obtained through trade with Colombia. The reptile below is of carved whale-tooth ivory covered with gold sheathing.

The 10-by-7-inch gold plaque at right is one of five found on the skeleton of the chief in Burial 11. In all, eight such plaques were recovered, each with perforations that allowed them to be sewn onto clothing as described in 16th-century Spanish reports.

In over-100-degree heat, the University Museum team poses with Panamanian laborers for a 1940 photo. Layers of soil had covered the graveyard, which is perhaps why it escaped Spanish attention. It is one of the few such sites that Spaniards and local graverobbers had not looted in their blind search for gold objects.

into it in ancient times." Still, only three documented attempts were made to mine the lake in the 16th and 17th centuries. Maybe it seemed too close, too easy an answer to the Spaniards. More likely, tranquil, lonely Lake Guatavita simply did not match their well-burnished vision of golden cities and gleaming temples.

The first assault on the lake took the form of an Indian bucket brigade organized by Hernán Pérez de Quesada, who in 1541 had commanded one of the earliest El Dorado expeditions. Sometime around 1545 Quesada stationed several hundred Indians a yard apart on the bank of the laguna and had them pass gourds of water up the slope to drain on the other side. Three months of this netted some 3,000 pesos' worth of gold objects.

Nearly 40 years passed before a Bogotá wine exporter named

Prussian naturalist Alexander von Humboldt explores the banks of the Orinoco during a five-year tour of the New World that began in 1799 and covered more than 6,000 miles. Turning a scientific eye on the quest for El Dorado, Humboldt concluded that there was no inland salt lake; it was nothing more than the Parima River at its flood stage.

Antonio de Sepúlveda attempted a follow-up. Granted a royal license to drain the lake, Sepúlveda had an Indian work force 8,000 strong cut a hillside trench deep enough to lower the water level 65 feet. From the mud thus laid bare his men plucked ornaments including "breastplates, a staff covered with gold plaques and an emerald the size of a hen's egg." Though encouraged, Sepúlveda was obliged to abandon the effort when a cave-in killed many of the workers, leaving behind a notch that can still be seen. In 1625 a group from a mining camp gained permission to drain the lake, with a proviso that up to half the profits would go to the king, but if they did any work it was not recorded.

No further efforts to mine the lake were made in the 17th and 18th centuries. Then, in 1801, the great pioneering natural scientist Alexander von Humboldt *(right)* visited the site, precipitating a new wave of interest. Humboldt accepted the story of the ceremony of the gilded man and identified steps hewn from the lakeside rock he said were used in the "ceremonial baptism." Humboldt also tried to estimate the treasure in the lake, calculating that if 1,000 pilgrims had lobbed five golden trinkets into the water annually for 100 years, the total value would be $300 million. A French scholar, however, apparently caught up in the fantasy of Guatavita's golden treasure, quickly revised this figure upward to $5.6 billion.

It was thus hardly surprising when a new lake drainer, a prominent Bogotá citizen named José Ignacio "Pepe" París, appeared in the altiplano in 1823 at the head of 16 investors. París's workers began cutting a new trench, but when a British naval captain named Charles Cochrane visited the lake he noticed that the water was eroding the trench's walls. He reinforced the channel with planks, but the shoring failed to keep it from crumbling. The water level eventually subsided by 10 feet but no farther, as seven successive canals caved in. Nothing if not persistent, París then decided to dig a tunnel below the level of the lake bed, but this too collapsed, killing several Indian laborers. Shares in París's company "diminished much in value," and the dogged Pepe finally quit sometime after 1826.

A generation later the focus shifted to Lake Siecha, a smaller but similarly circular lake not far from Guatavita. A channel almost 10 feet deep and 164 feet long lowered the level of Lake Siecha by about 10 feet in 1856 and exposed several gold objects, including a nine-ounce piece depicting what archaeologists believe to be the El Dorado ceremony itself *(page 6)*. This raised the possibility that Siecha and not Guatavita was the sacred lake and inspired a second attempt to drain Siecha in 1870. The venture ended when two men digging a 200-yard tunnel were asphyxiated.

Not until 1904 did any of the schemes devised to empty Lake Guatavita actually work, and this success was followed, perhaps inevitably, by yet another frustrating disappointment. An English company called Contractors Limited attracted 966 shareholders, many of them small investors, with a plan to drain the lake through a combination of a steam pump and a 437-yard tunnel through solid limestone to mid-lake. Sluices were to control the flow of water while mercury screens snagged any gold dust or precious objects before they escaped. Mules freighted heavy equipment, dynamite, and other tools and provisions into the cordillera. Amazingly, the idea worked. A German traveler who visited the dry lake bed in the summer of 1910 reported seeing an expanse of mud streaked with rivulets and small pools.

But the jubilation of the workers who had toiled several years to view the scene was short-lived. The muddy bottom, they discovered, was too soft to walk on. A day later the sun-baked mud was too hard to penetrate. Frustrated laborers picked up a number of gold objects including neck and nose ornaments, a golden helmet, an image of a goddess, and others, which were later auctioned in London, but nature foiled the entrepreneurs as thoroughly as it had balked the explorers of mountains, jungles, and llanos. In the few weeks it took to transport drilling gear to Guatavita, the hard mud plugged the sluices and tunnel and the spring-fed lake refilled. Contractors Limited sputtered on for a few more years before work stopped for good in 1914.

Latter-day Pérez de Quesadas and Pepe Paríses besieged the lake with increasingly sophisticated equipment in the 20th century. Divers descended into the ooze in heavy diving suits, draglines and clawed steel balls were hauled across the bottom, and metal detectors and suction pumps were tried—but Guatavita yielded scant additional treasure. In 1965 the Colombian government declared the lake a historical site and prohibited all further attempts to drain it.

The Muisca people who were living in the country surrounding Lake Guatavita and Bogotá when the Spaniards arrived had created an orderly, economically stable, and generally peaceful society based on highland farming, trade, and a metalworking skill developed over several centuries. The earliest Muisca radiocarbon dates, derived from charcoal found in gold artifacts, are from the sixth century AD. When the soldiers of Gonzalo Jiménez de Quesada marched into Muisca territory soon after Francisco Pizarro conquered the Incas in 1533, they found roughly a million Muiscas. Quesada's men systematically occupied one town after another, easily subduing warriors armed only with wooden swords and shields and javelin-like spears—

When news of a gunfight between graverobbers in a Colombian coastal jungle reached archaeologist Gilberto Cadavid, he immediately saw the implications: If looters were killing each other, it must be over a valuable site. From his post at the Colombian Institute of Anthropology in Santa Marta, he made inquiries. His hunch proved correct, and several months later, in March 1976, Cadavid mounted an expedition to unearth one of the

largest pre-Columbian enclaves ever found—the "lost city" of the Tairona, which he named Buritaca 200 for the nearby river and the number of excavated sites in the area.

The desire to escape warlike tribes and find a healthier climate with more-abundant rainfall had brought the Tairona people to the coastal mountains nearly a thousand years before the arrival of the Spaniards. The rain at 3,000 to 4,000 feet was sufficient for agriculture, and the altitude made for defensible towns. Indeed, for 75 years the Tairona were able to resist Spanish domination from their high perches, until in 1600 the Spaniards finally overwhelmed them and torched their villages.

Their very name would have attracted European attention, for in their native tongue the word *tairo* means goldworker. And so they were—producing exquisite, technically advanced work, such as the pendant of a stylized chieftain at right. The figure wears a bat mask and an elaborate headdress that displays two birds.

However much the metalworking prowess of the Tairona impressed the excavators, their engineering feats amazed them even more. The Indians had layered the high slopes with circular terraces like those in the photo at left. There they not only erected their houses but also planted corn, beans, peppers, avocados, sweet potatoes, fruit, manioc, and cotton. Scores of villages sprang up, inhabited by an estimated

300,000 people, some 3,000 of them in Buritaca itself.

These settlements consisted of anywhere from a few to several hundred round, wooden thatched-roof houses, about 14 to 39 feet in diameter, clustered around ceremonial structures. The stone-paved path shown at left is typical of the nearly 300 miles of roads and stairs linking scores of these towns. Stone-lined ditches, reservoirs, and underground sluices made up a drainage system that prevented erosion, a feat unmatched even today on Colombia's upland coffee plantations. Descendants of the Tairona, the Kogi, continue to live close by, preserving many of the ancient ways and giving archaeologists insight into the past.

they lacked the bows and poison-tipped arrows other tribes had. In the Bogotá valley the Spaniards beheld so many "magnificent buildings, houses and palaces of wood" that Quesada named the area Valle de los Alcázares, Valley of the Castles.

Independent Muisca farmers raised corn, tomatoes, manioc, beans, coca, various fruits, and the potato, a novelty to the Spaniards; "when cooked it is as soft as boiled chestnuts," Cieza de León wrote. The Muisca also made loaves of salt from deposits found in saline wells. The mineral and emeralds were the Indians' main trade commodities. Lacking pack animals and wheeled vehicles, they carried the items on foot to neighboring tribes and trade fairs. The priest Pedro Simón wrote of bazaars held every four days where peoples of various "provinces and nations" exchanged goods including gold—for which, ironically, the Muisca lacked a natural source.

Pedro Simón described the severe strictures and sacrifices that were part of Muisca life. The cacique, or ruler, he wrote, served a six-year apprenticeship during which he could not eat meat, enjoy sex, or see the sun—he went outside only at night. Priests endured 12 years of similar deprivation. Muisca traders eagerly sought young boys who were raised as slaves and sacrificed to the sun god when they reached puberty.

The Spaniards also described a dedicatory custom that almost defies belief: Young girls, they wrote, were sometimes used as building material in the construction of temples and palaces—dropped into postholes, covered with earth, and crushed to death by poles driven into the holes. But archaeologists excavating the ruins of a palace at Tiahuanaco, the capital of an empire that governed the southern Andes from AD 500 to 1000, have uncovered clues that the practice was carried out in a somewhat different way. Human remains discovered under the structure's corners and entrance were found not crushed but in flexed, seated positions, with copper bracelets, beaded lapis lazuli collars, and other spectacular grave goods.

Back arched, this alert little Muisca feline, less than an inch long, is probably a jaguar, the fierce predator of South America. Its extended tail—a product of the excess metal remaining from the casting channel—and long whiskers give the gold-and-copper cat a dragonlike appearance.

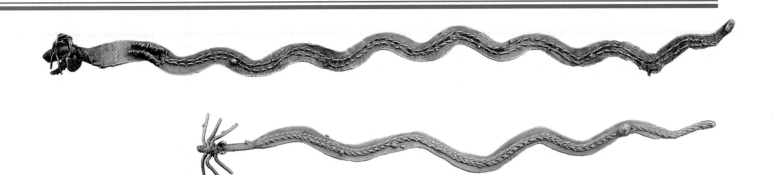

When Muisca chiefs went to war, Cieza de León wrote, they wore great golden crowns and thick gold armbands and carried banners "covered with small pieces of gold, like stars." They acquired the gold from trading partners elsewhere in Colombia and developed their own goldworking techniques, including all the important methods then known. Their work was stylistically distinctive, usually flat and sometimes triangular in shape *(page 77),* often bearing details with a storytelling content.

Archaeologists believe that the knowledge of goldworking techniques in South and Central America moved south to north, from Peru to Mexico over perhaps 2,000 years (map, *page 13).* The greatest variety in style and method occurred in Colombia, where goldsmiths were important enough, according to the chronicler Juan de Castellanos, that they were dispatched from their home villages to work in outlying areas.

To the Spaniards, of course, gold was material wealth, but it meant something else to the Indians. To them, as the Colombian anthropologist and ethnographer Gerardo Reichel-Dolmatoff has written, gold and emeralds "were divine generative forces, cosmic forces which guaranteed survival, food, procreation. Gold and emeralds formed the foundations of a transcendental world view. Even if they were a measure of a man's wealth, it was a wealth that belonged to divine forces."

Most of the slender archive of information about the beliefs and behavior of Colombian Indians comes not from archaeology but from descriptions by Spanish chroniclers, which can be a dubious source. Scientific study has been hampered by the early extinction of many tribes, their lack of a written language, and perhaps most important, centuries of pillage by huaqueros. The Tairona, an accomplished people who fought the Spaniards for most of a century before they were finally subdued in 1600, are an exception. Tairona lands have yielded more than 200 archaeological sites including irrigation canals, stone roads and bridges, and sizable towns *(pages 30-31)*. Moreover, a contemporary people—the Kogi—trace their ancestry to the Tairona. Kogi customs suggest that Tairona women enjoyed a status of equality rare among South American natives—marriages were monogamous, and women were permitted to remarry and to own and inherit property.

Among the gold-rich Quimbaya and other peoples of the Cauca River valley, by contrast, a man could have as many wives as he could afford. An aggressive people who the Spaniards claimed raised some children as a food source, the Catío built fortified houses with logs on the roofs that could be dropped on invaders. The conquistadors described a festival during which Quimbaya men and women, under the influence of a narcotic, lined up opposite each other and, at a signal, attacked one another with clubs and spears.

Strength and ferocity were celebrated in Indian legends. It was said that Pijao warriors—the cannibalistic southern neighbors of the Quimbaya—could swim the Magdalena River with a prisoner in each hand. One chief was described as so powerful that he strung 150 men on his spear. Another tale held that the Pijao were partial to Spanish flesh, except for friars, whom they regarded as poisonous.

But in the end, one custom, more than any other, set greedy hearts pounding—the Indian manner of burial. When a chief was interred, Pedro Simón wrote, "in the eyes, nostrils, ears, mouth and navel they put emeralds and pieces of gold, according to the wealth of each one, and around the neck they put discs of the same." Tradition also dictated that "the women and slaves who loved him best" be buried with their lord. Such practices inspired the institutionalized, father-to-son business of graverobbing, which began with the Spaniards and became an established if never quite honorable profession in the 19th century and continues unabated to this day.

But even the most avid of treasure seekers have not been able to thwart the efforts of archaeologists in South America entirely. Indeed, driven by a desire to know more about the people told of in the Spanish accounts and to understand better the ancient goldworking cultures, archaeologists and other scholars have succeeded in shedding light not just on Colombian and Ecuadoran history but also on that of Peru, and not only on the days of the conquistador but back many centuries earlier as well—to the age of a remarkable culture known as the Chavin.

MANIPULATING THE SUN

In their lust for gold, the seekers after El Dorado all too often were blind to the metallurgical achievements of the Indians. Yet when the German artist Albrecht Dürer beheld treasures sent from the New World by Hernán Cortés to the Holy Roman Emperor Charles V in 1520, he marveled at their intricacy and beauty. "Never in all my born days," he wrote, "have I seen anything that warmed my heart as much as these things."

The pieces that so captivated Dürer were the products of a metalworking tradition that was then more than 2,000 years old. Long before Spanish ships sailed into American waters, Indian smiths had mastered virtually all of the basic techniques employed by their European counterparts, including lost-wax casting, soldering, sheathing, plating, and inlaying. Starting as early as the 10th century BC with the Chavin of Peru's Andes and spreading north into Central America and beyond, metalworkers had learned to combine soft, malleable gold with silver, copper, and platinum into strong alloys. They knew how to gild, silver, and chemically manipulate metals to alter their colors and surface textures. And with an aesthetic sophistication that matched their technical prowess, they could hammer gold into leaflike thinness, press intricate designs into the sheets, and join the pieces into compelling and complex forms.

To the pre-Columbian Indians, gold was a sacred metal that incorporated the sun's creative energy. Transformed into objects of beauty, it transcended its earthly origins to become a tangible expression of status, wealth, political power, and divinity. The solar diadem pictured above, a masterpiece of cut gold sheet work that once adorned the forehead of a priest or ruler of the La Tolita culture sometime between 600 BC and AD 400, would have conferred on its wearer the very radiance of the life-giving sun.

THE SIMPLE TOOLS OF THE MASTERS

Remarkably, ancient America's metalsmiths achieved their extraordinary degree of technical proficiency using only the most basic equipment. "These inconvenient contrivances," as Spanish chronicler Garcilaso de la Vega condescendingly described the Indians' tools, consisted principally of braziers and crucibles made of clay, and smooth, hard stones employed as hammers and anvils.

Having no bellows to feed air to their fires, ancient American metalworkers used blowpipes instead. Channeling their breath onto burning charcoal, they raised temperatures to the levels necessary to melt gold dust and nuggets and to smelt raw copper from its ore.

A decoratively incised terra-cotta tube about four inches long was probably a mouthpiece fitted to one of the cane blowpipes utilized by goldsmiths in central Colombia's Muisca territory.

On a ceramic bowl made sometime between AD 100 and 800 during the period of Peru's Moche culture, the figures of three metalworkers blow through tubes into a dome-shaped brazier. Blowing simultaneously, several men could raise the temperature of a charcoal fire to between 1,800 and 2,300 degrees Fahrenheit.

Found along western Colombia's Cauca River, this simple clay crucible, about four and a half inches high, was used for melting gold. It was placed directly in the fire. The result was a small, button-shaped ingot, rounded on one face where the molten metal conformed to the vessel's curved bottom. The crucible's slightly flared rim may have allowed workers to lift it from the fire, perhaps with the aid of green branches.

Fashioned from stone, a cylindrical anvil and haftless egg-shaped hammer were used to pound metals into flat disks or plaques of sheet metal. Gonzalo Fernández de Oviedo, the Spanish king's supervisor of New World smelting opera-tions for nearly 20 years, from 1513 to 1532, described the anvils, which were usually around seven to eight inches in diameter, as "the size of a Majorcan cheese."

Typical of the tableware once reserved for chiefs, a semispherical gold bowl from Colombia's Calima culture—which flourished between the first and 12th centuries AD—was created by means of a technique called raising. To shape such a vessel, a smith hammered a flat, unadorned disk of sheet metal against a concave surface, gently pounding the center of the disk into the shape of a shallow saucer, then gradu-ally raising the sides by deepening the vessel through further pounding.

BEATING GOLD TO WAFER THINNESS

The production of many of the New World's most spectacular gold objects called for the beating of gold nuggets or, more commonly, precast ingots of a gold-and-copper alloy known as tumbaga into flat sheets. But because beating alters the microstructure of most metals—hardening them and making them prone to cracking—the smiths had to use a process called annealing to restore the sheets' malleability. They would bring the hammered metal to red heat in their charcoal fires, then plunge it into water to cool it before pounding it again. Once the metal had reached the desired thinness through repeated applications of this process, the hammered and annealed sheets were cut, bent, embossed, or pressed into or over molds to create the desired objects.

Discovered in southern Colombia, a mask of the copper-and-gold alloy tumbaga is a masterful example of the technique known as repoussé. In this process the smith would draw a design on a sheet of metal, allowing the lines to show on the other side, then turn the sheet over, place it on some yielding background material, and hammer it into a three-dimensional object. Once completed, the example of repoussé shown here was probably laid over a wooden mask and held in place with pins through the still-visible holes.

A ruler or priest of Peru's Chimu culture, which flourished between AD 900 and 1450, wore this gold collar and matching epaulets. The repeated motif depicting a figure grasping a human head in each hand is an embossed design, pressed into the metal from the opposite side with a carved stamp. The collar's dangling petal-like fringe was typical of Peruvian ceremonial jewelry, designed to shimmer with the sun's rays at the slightest movement.

JOINING PIECES OF METAL TOGETHER

As early as 200 BC, Andean smiths discovered the basic metalworking techniques of soldering and sweat welding. For soldering, they used an alloy with a low melting point, such as a gold-and-copper mix, to join two pieces of metal together; in sweat welding, they joined the pieces by carefully heating them. Both processes made possible the very fine work called granulation, in which tiny balls or thin wires of gold were fixed in place on a metal surface.

To assemble large or complex ornaments, the metalworkers also employed a host of mechanical methods. Among these were pinning, riveting, stapling, lacing with wires, and clinching, in which two edges were overlapped, folded over, and hammered down. Examples are reproduced on these two pages.

On a 13 ½-inch scepter found in a royal tomb at Peru's Sipán, a hollow trapezoidal finial of embossed sheet gold, its top masterfully soldered to its sides, is connected to a gold tube. The tube in turn is fitted to a cast silver handle.

Baring silver teeth, a turquoise-eyed, coral-whiskered opossum-like Moche figure nearly 15 inches long is assembled from separately made elements. Its repoussé gold head, legs, and tail were soldered together with a copper-silver alloy. A testament to the artisan's skill, ornamental disks still dangle from the creature's torso, attached to it by tiny wires.

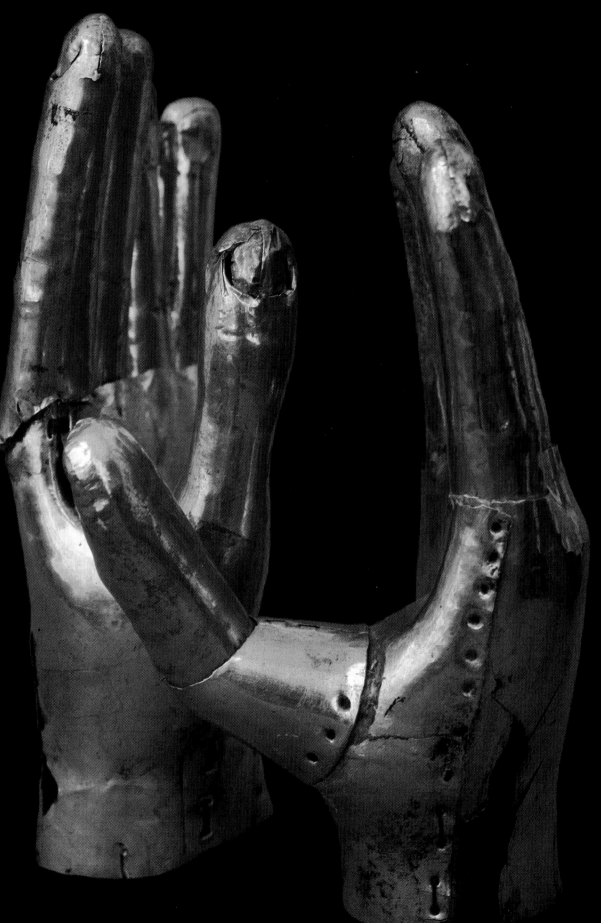

The hammered gold digits and palms on a pair of life-size ceremonial Moche gloves are connected to one another with small rivets and staples. Silver fingernails may once have been stapled to the fingertips through the tiny perforations still detectable there.

JEWELRY MODELED IN WAX

To create finely detailed pieces of jewelry and sculpture, the smiths used the lost-wax process. For small hollow objects, a clay core formed into a shape slightly smaller than the intended piece was covered with beeswax. The artisan then carved and molded the wax surface into an exact model of the finished object. The wax was enveloped in a thick casing of clay pierced with wooden pegs to hold the core in position. Finally, the clay mold was heated to melt out the wax, and molten metal was poured into the cavity to replicate the model.

To produce something called false filigree, the metalsmiths first made fine wax threads, perhaps rolling them by hand or extruding them through a nozzle into cold water. Then they built these into a lacy model. After gently encasing the model in clay, they used the lost-wax process to cast the piece.

Cast sometime between AD 400 and 800, a six-inch-long gold tortoise from Panama is a hollow container once probably used to hold a small quantity of lime. The lime would have been mixed with coca leaves and chewed for a mild but energizing narcotic effect.

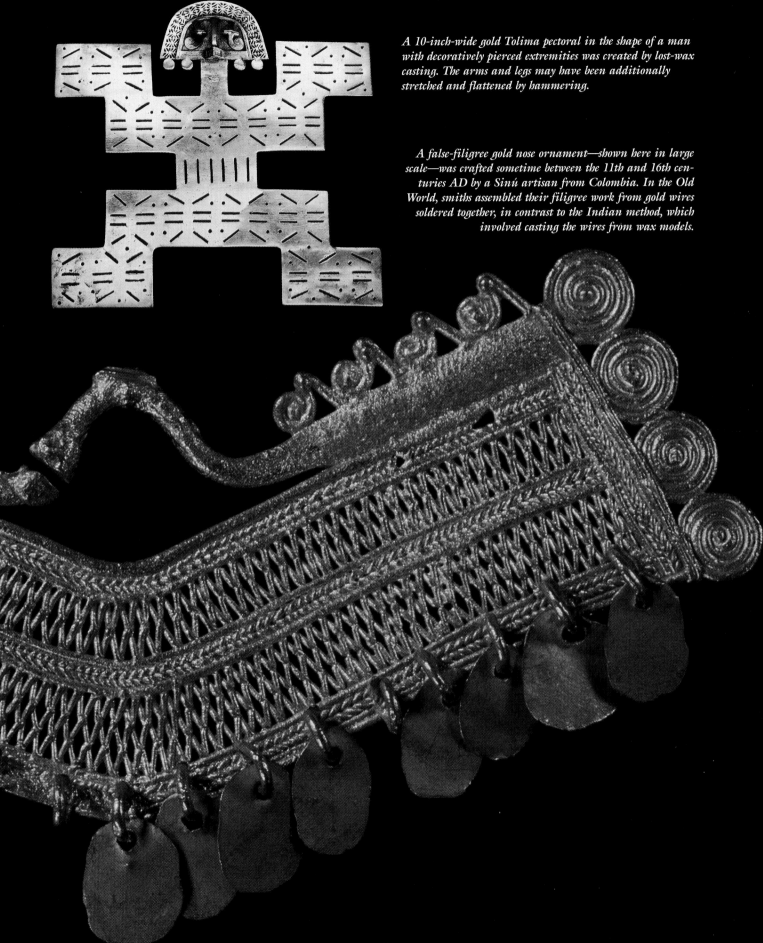

A 10-inch-wide gold Tolima pectoral in the shape of a man with decoratively pierced extremities was created by lost-wax casting. The arms and legs may have been additionally stretched and flattened by hammering.

A false-filigree gold nose ornament—shown here in large scale—was crafted sometime between the 11th and 16th centuries AD by a Sinú artisan from Colombia. In the Old World, smiths assembled their filigree work from gold wires soldered together, in contrast to the Indian method, which involved casting the wires from wax models.

43

THE ILLUSORY GLEAM OF ALLOYS

Much of the Indian metallurgist's art was devoted to creating gold or silver surfaces on objects that contained relatively little amounts of either metal.

Items made of tumbaga, the commonly used alloy, were frequently subjected to a technique known as depletion gilding *(opposite, below)*, a chemical process that stripped copper molecules from the surface, leaving the superficial luster of gold on objects whose actual gold content might be as low as 15 percent.

Electrochemical replacement plating *(below)* deposited thin layers of gold or silver on copper objects. In fusion coating, the copper items were dipped in a bath of molten silver or gold. A simpler way to gild was to take gold foil and carefully beat it onto the piece.

Beads on two necklaces taken from the grave of a Moche lord at Sipán were apparently gilded by electrochemical replacement plating. This called for dissolving gold in an acidic solution of salt and corrosive minerals. When a copper object was dipped into the solution, an electrochemical exchange took place, with some of the gold adhering to the copper as a bit of the copper itself dissolved and entered the solution.

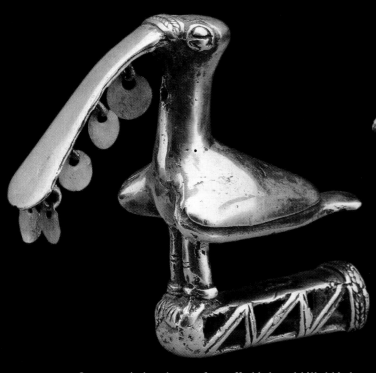

Once attached to the top of a staff, this broad-billed bird effigy has the characteristic pinkish glow of the copper-and-gold alloy tumbaga, one of the principal metals used in pre-Hispanic times. Tumbaga was favored in large part because of the different shades smiths could achieve by varying the proportions of the components. The Indians apparently regarded the combination of metals as a fertile merging of male and female elements—the yellow gold representing male potency and the reddish copper femininity.

Composed of links cast by the lost-wax process, an opulent tumbaga necklace from Tairona, Colombia, exhibits the glitter achieved through depletion gilding. Each link was heated until the copper on its surface combined with oxygen in the air to produce a scaly coating. The links were then bathed in an acidic solution of plant juices or stale urine to dissolve the scale, thus removing the copper on the surface and leaving a spongy, gold-enriched layer that could be polished or burnished to a fine golden sheen.

WORKING WITH UNYIELDING PLATINUM

The ore-bearing gravels found in the rivers draining into the Pacific Ocean from the mountains of Ecuador and Colombia are liberally mixed with gray-white specks of pure platinum—an exceptionally hard metal the 17th-century Spaniards found so obdurately unworkable that they discarded it as quickly as they could separate it from its accompanying gold. Yet nearly 1,000 years earlier, La Tolita metalworkers had invented an ingenious process—which was not to be duplicated by Europeans for another 1,500 years—that allowed them to put the metal to striking decorative use.

Because platinum has an exceptionally high melting point—3,000 degrees Fahrenheit versus 1,950 degrees Fahrenheit for pure gold—it could not be melted by any of the methods then available. So the Indian smiths combined platinum grains and gold dust and heated the mixture over a charcoal fire. As the gold liquefied, it bonded with the particles of platinum, forming a molten mass that, after cooling down, was then alternately hammered and reheated to eventually become a workable material that could be fashioned into small objects.

Incorporating the metalworking techniques of repoussé, filigree, and soldering, this La Tolita pectoral was produced from a gold sheet. The figure and the balls around the edge are platinum covered. Besides burnishing an item made of a gold-platinum alloy to bring out the platinum, smiths could clad gold with grains of the metal, heat the gold so it fused with them, and then polish the surface to make the platinum gleam.

A brood...
of he...
Ecuador...
stares blankl...
platin...

THE CHAVIN: BUILDERS OF GIANT WONDERS

More than six decades ago, workers were enlarging a water reservoir near the town of Chongoyape in northern Peru's arid Lambayeque Valley when they uncovered three disintegrated skeletons some 10 feet below the surface. Except for traces of cinnabar, with which the corpses may have been painted red in preparation for burial, two of the three were unadorned. But the third—determined later to be that of a woman—had been laid out in regal splendor. Clustered about her remains was a trove of gold objects, including 19 decorative snail shells, 66 beads, 11 pottery beads encased in the precious metal, and a headband, seven and a quarter inches in diameter, fashioned from a thin sheet of gold. One of its ends had been cut into four strips, each of which ended in reptilian heads. A pair of gold gorgets, or pendants—one depicting a crab, the other featuring a fanged monster surrounded by intertwined serpents—and delicate rings of gold lay nearby. Pins of gold and silver were found as well. They had perhaps fastened a cloak or held the woman's hair.

The pieces were to pass through many hands before a museum in New York purchased them. Then word of the find spread. Archaeologists came running to see the collection, not only because it had remained intact, but also because of the dramatic way it altered scholars' understanding of the history of northern Peru: Until then,

Assuming the fierceness of a jaguar, a shaman—or priest—under the influence of an intoxicant exhibits the wide-eyed stare and dripping mucus that heralded the beginning of a trance. The sculpture is one of a series that once studded a wall of the Chavin de Huantar temple complex in Peru.

there had been no indication that the region had been occupied for more than a few centuries before the Spaniards' arrival. Yet the style of two ceramic bottles among the funeral goods matched that of vessels found elsewhere in Peru, indicating that the burial had taken place more than two millennia earlier—around 400 BC—when a culture known as the Chavin was at its peak.

Though still unknown to many people around the globe, Chavin ranks among the world's great formative civilizations—not unlike Sumer in Mesopotamia, the Olmec in Central America, or the Shang dynasty in China. It is remembered today, in part, for its impressive earth-and-stone religious structures. But if these monuments survived to show that there once was a group with the organizational ability and genius to construct them, too little was known for too long about the people themselves.

Stone items recovered from the burial—a plate and cup for offering food and chicha, or corn beer, and a spoon suitable for inhaling hallucinogenic snuff—implied that the woman and her two companions may have been practitioners of some magico-religious rites. Yet what sort of faith had inspired their ceremonies remained unclear, as did the symbolic importance of the deceased's more lustrous grave goods.

Chongoyape itself offered too few clues to solve these mysteries. For more information, researchers would have to look some 300 miles inland, high on the eastern slopes of the Cordillera Blanca in the Andes Mountains. There, near the confluence of the Mosna and Huachecsa Rivers, lay the ruins of one of ancient Peru's premier religious centers—Chavin de Huantar, after which the ancient culture has been named. From humble and obscure beginnings, probably in the first half of the first millennium BC, the site had grown into an imposing temple whose white granite walls stood 50 feet high and whose reputation spread far beyond the surrounding terrain. By 500 BC, it had become a destination for pilgrims from the country's remote coastal and highland valleys.

Much of Chavin de Huantar's drawing power stemmed from its awe-inspiring architecture and monumental sculptural details. In its early phases the temple consisted of three enormous platform mounds arranged in a U-shape atop a pedestal of cyclopean stone blocks. Gazing upon its massive walls, worshipers beheld a bas-relief frieze of anthropomorphic creatures, spotted jaguars, writhing serpents, and wild birds of prey, below which projected a row of monstrous human heads *(page 48)* sculpted from stone blocks weighing as much as half a ton each. Tenons at the back of the heads fit snugly into mortise joints in the masonry, creating the illusion that the sculptures were floating some 30 feet above ground. A frieze depicting similar figures—jaguars and exotically costumed humans—adorned the sunken, circular plaza that lay between the three mounds. A white granite staircase climbed from the plaza up to the temple's summit.

In time Chavin de Huantar's massive structures proved too small, and laborers doubled the size of the southern mound and added terraced platforms and sunken rectangular courtyards southeast of the circular plaza *(page 59)*. A portico framed by black and white pillars graced the front of the southern wing, which is referred to as the New Temple, whose top now became the focal point of the public ceremonies.

Pilgrims gathering on the New Temple's main plaza would have had a commanding view of the ritual platform. No exterior staircase surmounted this new structure; the mound's apparently inaccessible summit was instead approached by a labyrinthine network of interior passages and stairways. Garbed in fine cotton, woolen, or feathered tunics and adorned with gold nose ornaments, earspools, and headdresses, Chavin de Huantar's priests must have elicited considerable wonder when, as if by magic, they emerged on top.

Scholars speculate that worshipers departed the complex carrying away with them mementos of the celebrations to venerate at home. Examples of these ritual objects—including clay friezes, painted textiles, and hammered gold plaques and figurines featuring animal gods executed in the same style that characterized Chavin de Huantar's fearsome, mammoth sculptures—have been discovered along Peru's coast and throughout the highlands by archaeologists and *huaqueros* alike.

One of Peru's most respected scholars is archaeologist Julio C. Tello. To his discerning eye, the gorget representing the intertwined serpents from the Chongoyape woman's burial echoed stylistically the snakes chiseled on Chavin de Huantar, which was about 280 miles to the northwest. That the Chongoyape gold also shared symbolic or metaphoric elements with objects found elsewhere argued for the existence of what Tello and later scholars dubbed a horizon, an era of marked innovation and sweeping cultural integration. But the culture's scope was what made it so amazing. Despite the seeming barriers posed by Peru's mountains, Chavin culture from about 900 to 200 BC had apparently spread throughout a wide region. Well over a thousand years later the Incas would subjugate the diverse residents of the country's barren, coastal desert, glacier-capped Andes, and jungle-clad lowlands by relentless armed conquest, but no such force lay behind the spread of Chavin civilization. Its expansion, which marks a period known as the Early Horizon, appears to have been accomplished by means of a far less violent agency—the power of religious belief.

The thousands of Chavinoid artifacts unearthed so far remain persuasive proof of this spread of influence. Made up of religiously charged pottery, exquisitely crafted gold trinkets, and finely woven textiles, they apparently served as the Chavin culture's medium of spiritual exchange. Beautiful to behold and imbued with special meaning, these objects may have once served to proclaim the wearer's allegiance to a cult whose gods transcended regional limits.

Chavin culture, crystallizing what apparently had long been in the air in the Andean region, manifested itself in other diverse ways. In the religious realm, it left a lasting mark with its development of dual notions for the worldly and otherworldly realms and its association of gold and silver with divine principles. On a more down-to-earth level, its emphasis on communal labor and preference for the use of masonry in high-status public architecture presaged even bigger works projects to come. And in its reliance on irrigation for agriculture and its use of llamas as beasts of burden, it merged, modified, and spread existing patterns that would be followed for centuries. Indeed, Tello theorized that Chavin culture was like the trunk of an enormous tree out of which grew the innumerable and tangled branches of Peru's later cultures.

Drawing on the fruits of decades of further exploration by Peruvian, North American, and Japanese archaeologists, scholars today regard Tello's metaphor as somewhat of an overstatement. They know what he did not: that the Peruvian practice of building grand ceremonial centers dates back more than two millennia before Chavin de Huantar to 3000 BC—an era roughly contemporaneous with the royal pyramids of Egypt's Old Kingdom. Because more than a thousand years would pass from this time until the first pottery appeared in Peru, archaeologists refer to the period as the Preceramic.

An aerial view of the Early Horizon fortress of Chankillo, located high above the Casma Valley, shows it surrounded by a series of thick walls. Hilltop fortresses like this began to appear during post-Chavin times, when hostilities erupted between small-scale groups within local valleys.

Even without pottery, however, it was far from being an age without splendid achievements, as is evidenced by the ruins of its early ceremonial structures.

Probably built to appease deities believed to control a capricious climate, the early pre-Chavin monuments stand in sharp contrast to the day-to-day situation of most coastal inhabitants at the time. They lived in primitive shelters made of ocean-worn stones roofed with whale bone, and they consumed anchovies, sardines, and shellfish. Other shore dwellers resided farther inland in houses of fieldstone, adobe, and clay and supplemented their marine diet with plant foods coaxed from the alluvial soils of nearby riverbanks. Highlanders, by contrast, subsisted mostly on deer, guinea pigs, and wild edibles and, if there was adequate rainfall, potatoes, corn, and beans.

In good years, coastal peoples and mountain dwellers alike ate well enough. But as often as five times a century, climate studies show, a disturbance in the normal sea and wind currents along the coast causes a phenomenon known as El Niño, which as recently as 1973 nearly ruined Peru's commercial fishing industry. Ocean temperatures rise by more than six degrees Fahrenheit, and precipitation patterns over land are drastically altered. Unable to tolerate the warmer waters, the microscopic plants that form the basis of the ocean food chain die off, and fish, sea mammals, and birds migrate or perish. The altered wind patterns bring torrential rains and catastrophic flooding to the low-lying coast and, ironically, killing drought to the highlands.

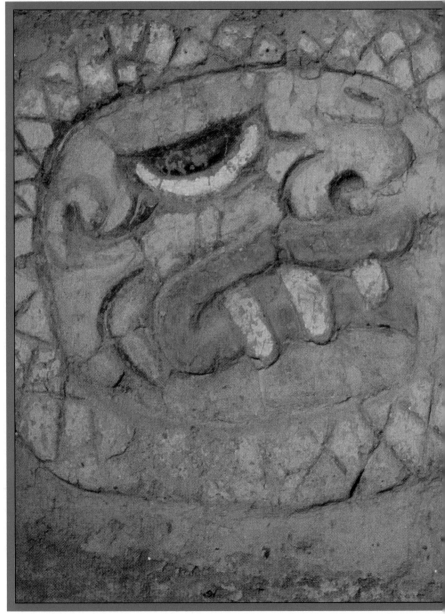

In the face of such hardship, Peru's ancient peoples would doubtlessly have been eager to propitiate the gods who they believed controlled their homeland's rains and fragile ecosystems. They did so, archaeologists believe, by gathering to feast, dance, and conduct public ceremonies atop circular or rectangular stone platforms that were the precursors of later temples. Sometimes acres in extent and open to the elements, such centers involved intensive communal planning as well as phenomenal expenditures of physical labor. North American archaeologist Thomas Patterson has calculated that the largest of the Preceramic structures—El Paraíso, in the Chillón River valley just north of Lima—covered no less than 140 acres and incorporated some 100,000 tons of stone.

Remarkably, such mammoth bids for divine succor grew ever more spectacular over the years. Between 1800 and 900 BC, the time preceding the Early Horizon and known to archaeologists as the Initial Period, a new type of ceremonial architecture appeared at various locations in Peru's central coastal valleys. Even larger and more elaborate than the Preceramic centers, these complexes already incorporated the basic design features that would distinguish Chavin de Huantar—three truncated pyramids arranged in a U formation with steep staircases connecting the central rectangular plaza to the top of each mound.

Archaeologists have located some 20 of these imposing centers along a 125-mile stretch of coast from south of Lima to the Supe River valley to the north. Curiously, nearly all face away from the Pacific; their open ends point east instead, toward the headwaters of the desert rivers in the faraway Andes. Coupled with the impressive dimensions of these U-shaped centers—from which archaeologists have inferred the communal labors of more than 1,000 persons—the riverine orientation offers scholars a valuable clue. The position seems to indicate that by 1800 BC or so, coastal peoples no longer relied exclusively on simple fishing and flood-plain agriculture for their survival, but practiced large-scale canal irrigation as well. Rituals conducted on these grand structures, it is believed, probably centered on the highland rains that replenished the coastal rivers, the source of irrigation waters.

One of the most extensively studied of the enormous complexes, Garagay, today lies largely hidden under the modern city of Lima, five miles from the ocean in the lower Rímac River valley. The surviving section measures 40 acres in extent, more than half of which constitutes the original central plaza. Initial exploration of the site, begun in 1974 by archaeolo-

A conservator carefully injects a preservative under the clay surface of a painted relief at Garagay to stabilize the sculpture and prevent further deterioration. Regarded as having spider attributes by some scholars, the beast is one of several that decorate the central atrium of a temple at this pre-Chavin site.

gists William Isbell of the United States and Rogger Ravines of Peru, turned up a near-vertical stairway leading from the plaza to the top of the central mound, 75 feet above. There a passageway opened onto a recessed atrium. Badly damaged by erosion and the erection of an ill-placed television antenna, little of the ceremonial space remained. But searching directly beneath it, the archaeologists discovered an older atrium almost 80 feet square, which they named the Middle Temple.

Stairways flanked with pilasters stood along three of the Middle Temple's five-foot-high walls, and in the floor, circular pits large enough to accommodate wooden posts suggested that there may have been some sort of roof overhead. Sculpted images of monstrous figures decorated the temple walls *(pages 54-55)*. Modeled in fine clay and painted with mineral-based pigments in vivid shades of yellow, red, pink, white, and grayish blue, each bore human features and some possessed fangs. According to at least one archaeologist, spiderlike attributes are also discernible.

Both the teeth and the possible spider elements are thought to cast light on the type of ceremonies that were performed at Garagay. Preconquest Indians reportedly employed spiders to predict rainfall and other matters, and in Inca times, a special class of priests called *paccharícuc* routinely used spiders to foretell the future. The protruding fangs of many of Garagay's figures probably reflect the age-old veneration of South and Central American Indians for the jaguar, the supreme predator of the lowland jungles and the animal avatar of the shaman. The Indians regarded the cat as possessing mystical powers, akin to those of the spider. Shamans, assuming jaguar characteristics during transformation ceremonies, supposedly drew upon the jaguar's powers to divine the future and control events *(pages 75-83)*.

In two small circular pits located in the floor of the Middle Temple, archaeologists Isbell and Ravines found further evidence of Garagay's religious significance—a pair of doll-like clay figurines. Probably left as offerings, each had been wrapped in cotton thread and painted to show large, wide-open eyes and enormous upper canine teeth. Strapped on the back of one of the figures were two large spines of San Pedro cactus, a night-blooming, columnar plant native to the Peruvian highlands. Shamans have long prized the cactus because its flesh contains the hallucinogen mescaline. Early Spanish sources indicate that holy men relied on hallucinogens to assume jaguar traits as the prelude to their performing supernatural rites. And even today, shamans among the Guahibo Indians of Colombia—appropriately attired in a jaguar pelt and a crown of the cat's claws—regularly snuff vision-inducing powder from a jaguar bone as part of a transformation ritual.

Such ancient shamans or priest-chieftains, it is thought, instigated, planned, and directed the construction and ceremonial use of Garagay and other coastal religious centers. Yet their authority was not political; it derived apparently from their religious eminence. As mediators between humans and the forces of nature, they alone would have possessed the power to set the agricultural calendar and to expunge the human offenses that were thought to rile the gods and invite disaster. As a result, the holy men enjoyed phenomenal prestige and were able to influence both group behavior and the distribution of goods and labor.

Judging from the absence of elite burials at the U-shaped complexes and the symbolic, rather than commemorative, character of the temple art, archaeologists theorize that the shamans worked to achieve the good of the community, not personal gain. Surplus riches were apparently used to reinforce their authority and to promote the cult's success by means of more elaborate rituals, fancier stonework and sculpture, and other public works. At Garagay, for example, Isbell and Ravines have uncovered indications that expansion and renovation occurred throughout the complex's 800-year-long history. Portions of the frieze in the Middle Temple, for example, revealed as many as 10 layers of paint, each meticulously matched in color and texture to the one before.

Sometime around 900 BC, however, the great coastal centers began to decline. Repairs to the stone-and-adobe mounds ceased, and some complexes seem to have been deserted altogether. Even new construction appears to have halted in mid-effort. Archaeologists excavating at Las Haldas, about 200 miles north of Garagay, discovered that only half the stairs leading from the central plaza to the pyramid's summit had been plastered before the complex was abruptly abandoned. Soon thereafter villagers erected crude huts on what had been a sunken circular court in the plaza and tossed their household refuse onto the unfinished staircase. No further construction was ever undertaken.

Such signs hint of a profound crisis, one that may have been ecological in origin. After more than 700 years of devotion to their

religious centers, the peoples of Peru's coastal valleys abandoned their homes and moved farther inland, where they now began constructing settlements on flattened hilltops. The North American archaeologist David J. Wilson has identified 21 of these citadels, many bordered by protective-looking terraces and stone walls, clustered about the middle and upper valley of the Santa River, about 200 miles north of Lima.

Curiously, highlanders, by all indications, were spared the upheavals that contributed to the displacement of the lowlanders at the end of the Initial Period. By contrast, their ceremonial centers seem not to have been abandoned or in any way defiled, and unlike their displaced brethren, the mountain dwellers apparently saw no need to

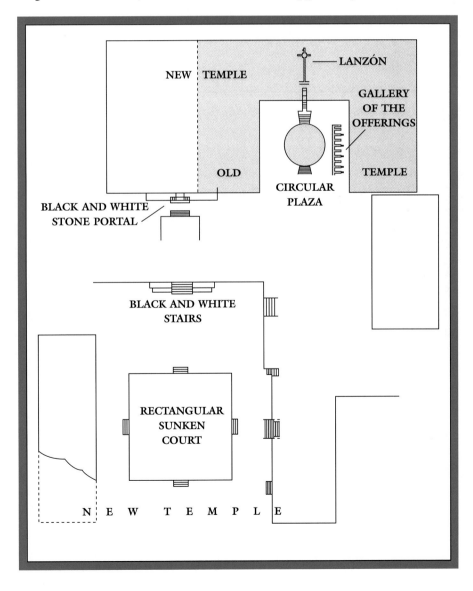

Nestled at the bottom of a steep valley at the junction of two rivers (left) on the eastern slope of the Andes Cordillera Blanca, the U-shaped, truncated pyramidal platforms of Chavin de Huantar's temple complex survive as ruins. The area within the square diagrammed at right shows the Old Temple, the two parts of the greatly expanded New Temple, as well as the locations of the site's other major features. The Old Temple's labyrinthine interior housed the large stone idol of the Chavin deity known as the Lanzón.

fortify their settlements. Indeed, they constructed several new complexes whose spiritual vigor seemed to increase with time. Among them was Chavin de Huantar itself.

By about 500 BC Chavin de Huantar had emerged as one of the most impressive ceremonial complexes in the north-central highlands and the north and central coast. According to North American anthropologist Richard L. Burger, few sites in the Andes were better situated; it lay close to the natural transportation routes linking the coast, mountains, and tropical lowlands. Only 10 snow-free passes intersect the Cordillera Blanca, Peru's lofty continental divide. Chavin de Huantar is in the cradle of one of these, where the east-flowing Mosna and north-flowing Huachecsa Rivers meet and run into the mighty Marañón River, forming a natural corridor east. Not only would travelers have frequented such a route for convenience, Burger theorizes, but it is probable that they would have considered it providential as well: Traditional Andean culture holds the spot at which two rivers or paths join to be ritually powerful or blessed.

Such themes of duality are reflected in the monumental structures of Chavin de Huantar itself. In its broad design, scholars say, the temple probably derived from the earlier U-shaped ceremonial structures found on the coast. But as can be seen in the tropical imagery and metaphorical symbolism associated with the complex's triad of stone gods, the architectural embellishments were different. These decorations represented a unique fusion of influences from the surrounding highlands, the Amazon basin to the east, and the coastal area to the west.

Known as the Lanzón, or lance, because of its lancelike shape, an effigy of the chief deity of the time, the Smiling God, stands in a cruciform chamber in the interior of Chavin de Huantar's old temple *(page 61)*. A two-ton, 15-foot-tall shaft of white granite, it bears the finely chiseled image of the half-human, half-feline god. Writhing snakes form the deity's hair, claws take the place of toes and fingers, and enormous, curved fangs project from the mouth. A mediator of opposites, the Smiling God holds his right hand in a raised position, and his left down at his side.

Images of two other Chavin deities were found in the temple's open spaces. A local farmer named Timoteo Espinosa discovered one in 1840 while cultivating fields in front of the structure. An engraved slab of granite as tall as a man, it portrays the fanged Staff

This drawing shows the clawed and fanged Staff God, a major deity of the Chavin during their later period, incised on the six-foot-tall slab of highly polished granite known as the Raimondi Stone, from Chavin de Huantar. Curiously, the carving emphasizes the tall headdress, which takes up more than two-thirds of the work.

God wearing an elaborate headdress of serpents and bearing the two cactuslike staffs that are the deity's emblem. Unaware of its historic significance, Espinosa used the monolith as a table and occasionally as a grinding stone. Thirty-three years later, Italian geographer Antonio Raimondi rediscovered the artifact and arranged for it to be transported to Lima, an undertaking that required the widening of a road by blasting. Now known as the famous Raimondi Stone, it resides in the National Museum of Archaeology in Lima.

Julio Tello unearthed the third deity of the Chavin pantheon some distance from the temple. Incised on a pointed shaft of granite were two fantastic caimans, or South American crocodilians, ornately garlanded with chili peppers, gourds, peanuts, and manioc roots, a rich source of carbohydrates. In traditional Andean lore, the caiman is venerated as the bestower of these and other food crops. Its dual image on the shaft suggested to Tello two different aspects of the same deity: one representing the rainy season and vegetative growth and the other signifying the dry season and the harvest. Like the Smiling God, the Caiman God—as represented on what would become known as the Tello Obelisk—seemed concerned with maintaining a balance between opposites.

Chavin de Huantar's architects, it appears, were intent on incorporating dual principles—one for the natural realm, the other for the supernatural—into the design of what is perhaps the center's most dramatic structural feature: the monumental staircase leading to the New Temple's main plaza. Faced on one side with sparkling white feldspar and on the other with black limestone, the staircase

Aptly named the Lanzón because of its lancelike shape (above), this 15-foot-tall granite sculpture is incised on both sides with an image of the principal deity of the Old Temple at Chavin de Huantar. The drawing of the work flattens out the design so the figure's balefully upturned eyes and feline fangs can be seen clearly. Holding one hand up and the other down, the god assumes a pose suggestive of his role as mediator of opposites.

exemplified the coexistence of contrasting elements: night and day, dark and light.

But as much as the public spaces reflected notions of balance, Chavín de Huántar's interior—a maze of lightless passageways and subterranean galleries—seemed designed to disorient the uninitiated. The ritual heart of the old temple lay in the vaulted 45-foot-long chamber that still houses the sacred Lanzón. Entry to this area, known as the Gallery of the Lanzón, was through a vestibule hidden behind the temple's ceremonial staircase. A three-foot-wide passageway led from the vestibule to the chamber, whose only light might have come from wall-mounted resin torches. At the center of the gallery, facing east, stands the Smiling God. Like an axis connecting the heavens, earth, and underworld, the shaft pierces both the floor and ceiling of the chamber.

Careful sleuthing by a series of archaeologists has revealed that the Lanzón's axial orientation fulfilled functional as well as symbolic purposes. Tello discovered a smaller cruciform gallery directly above the Gallery of the Lanzón. In the floor of this chamber, penetrated by the sharp tip of the idol below, Tello happened on an opening covered by a removable slab. Through this portal, the archaeologist surmised, Chavín de Huántar's priests could have made offerings to the Lanzón, perhaps by pouring some sacred liquid into a small channel that had been chiseled into the deity's top. Nearby Tello discovered a grisly clue that the libation may have been human blood: a finger bone that had been carefully carved with the temple's strange iconography.

Scholars have suggested other purposes for the opening above the Lanzón. Archaeologist Thomas Patterson, for instance, noticed that by speaking into the hole from the upper gallery, he could make the Lanzón appear to talk. This, he suggested, would have permitted the temple priests to stay out of sight while they filled the lower gallery with sonorous proclamations. That these pronouncements may have been the prophesies of the Lanzón, Burger suggests, can be gleaned by studying the late pre-Hispanic cult of Pachacamac, first described by conquistadors in AD 1534.

A vast ceremonial complex of adobe pyramids and platforms at the mouth of the Lurín River near Lima, Pachacamac, which survived as a religious center into conquest times, was the seat of a famed oracle. According to Spanish accounts, pilgrims bearing fine textiles, corn, dried fish, and gold came from all over Peru to seek counsel on

The white granite and black andesite pillars of this portal guard the approach to the eastern facade of the New Temple. The cylindrical columns are incised with fero-cious birds of prey. The columns and adjacent jambs still support portions of a two-piece lintel, also of black and white stone, that once spanned nearly 30 feet.

matters of planting, health, and personal fortune. Just to gain admittance to the lower plaza and the public ceremonies that were held there, pilgrims, nobles, and royalty alike had to fast for 20 days—an exercise that entailed abstaining from salt and chili peppers as well as sexual intercourse.

Worshipers wishing to ascend to the upper plaza had to maintain their fast for an entire year. Such devotion earned them the right to query the Pachacamac oracle, though not directly: Only temple priests were permitted to scale the pyramid's summit and consult the wooden idol. And even these august personages were not allowed to gaze upon the oracle itself, which was shrouded behind a cloth veil inside a windowless chamber. Answers from the oracle, as well as requests for offerings and tribute, were vocalized by the attending priest and relayed to the anxious petitioners waiting in the plaza below. Graduated terraces and hidden galleries at Chavin de Huantar suggest that a similar protocol may have applied to its ceremonial affairs. The majority of pilgrims, it is thought, would have ascended no higher than the New Temple's main plaza, the most public of the complex's sacred precincts.

The Lanzón's prophetic pronouncements, however, may not have been the only magical sounds filling the old temple. Beginning in 1966, Peruvian archaeologist Luís Lumbreras studied the ventilation and water-drainage systems of the structure. To provide the subterranean chambers and passageways with fresh air, the temple's builders installed an elaborate interconnected system of stone-lined ducts linking these spaces to the outside and to each other. They also created a parallel

Dressed stone blocks line a subterranean passageway inside the New Temple at Chavin de Huantar. A long series of such corridors and stairways connected the underground gallery complexes within the old and new temples.

system of hydraulic canals, ostensibly to drain away the torrential rains that inundate the valley five to eight months of the year. But the canals' drainage capacity, Lumbreras calculated, grossly exceeded that required for even the heaviest downpours; the ducts must have been constructed to serve an additional function—that is, to make the temple roar.

According to Lumbreras, the system may have worked like this: An underground canal would have channeled water from a high point on the Huachecsa River to the summit of the temple, some 540 yards away. From there the water fed into the structure's internal hydraulic system and rushed through a vertical conduit into the underlying honeycomb of stone-lined canals. Hurtling along narrow, sharply angled waterways, tumbling over stepped courses, and breaking against corners and protuberances, the water would have produced quite a lot of noise.

Communicated via the parallel air ducts to smooth-walled chambers whose dimensions conformed exactly to multiples of the wavelength of the sound, Lumbreras theorized, the noise may have been amplified eerily. The Gallery of the Lanzón, which is shaped like a megaphone, would have further increased the god's awe-inspiring roar, and temple priests could have modulated the pitch and direction of the sound by opening and closing the various air ducts like the valves of a giant trumpet.

To test his hypothesis, Lumbreras poured 105 gallons of water into conduits underlying the temple's central staircase. At once, a thunderous din enveloped the steps. Two clusters of what he called "sounding mouths" at the summit of the temple broadcast the roar from deep within the complex to the oracular chamber and to the grounds outside. The noise, of regular intensity and oscillating frequency, could never have been confused with that normally produced by rushing water. It sounded, Lumbreras wrote, like a multitude of hands applauding.

Lumbreras speculates that after passing through the old temple, the waters were discharged unseen into the Mosna River through a network of pipes that passed under the central plaza. Archaeological explorations have not been mounted to locate the conducting canal that would have ultimately carried these waters; nor has the hypothetical canal connecting the Huachecsa River and the temple summit yet been found. And some scholars, citing the devastating floods that have periodically struck the region over the last 2,500 years, doubt they ever will be, as any one of the deluges could have wiped out all traces of the conduits.

Lumbreras's theories, while unproven, are well within the bounds of possibility. A roaring temple would have immeasurably enhanced the supernatural authority already attached to the oracle of the Lanzón and to the bevy of priests attending it. Yet with or without its roar, Chavin de Huantar had features enough to have inspired a dedicated following. In the southwest corner of the temple's main plaza, for instance, archaeologists have turned up a 10-ton slab of limestone, the top of which bears a cluster of seven circular depressions. North American ethnographer Gary Urton has noted that these are arranged in a pattern strikingly similar to the Pleiades, a conspicuous group of stars in the constellation Taurus. Though the function of the stone can only be guessed at, Urton notes that to this day, Quechua farmers in Cuzco consult the star cluster before choosing the right time for planting and harvesting. The correlation, if one indeed exists, seems to suggest that many of the ceremonial events conducted on Chavin de Huantar's main plaza revolved around astronomical observations relating to the agricultural cycle, but scholars are unable to say for sure.

Inside a subterranean chamber located beneath the old temple's square court, north of the circular plaza, Marino Gonzales, the resident archaeologist at Chavin de Huantar, in 1966 discovered a collection of items that pilgrims taking part in such public activities may have brought to the temple as offerings. Known as the Galería de las Ofrendas, or Gallery of the Offerings, the storeroom comprised nine rectangular cells arranged to one side of a straight, narrow passageway that was more than 80 feet long. Each cell housed a different type of article: In the first cell were pottery bottles, in the third bowls and plates, in the sixth globular jars, and in the ninth carved stone objects such as a bear-shaped mortar and a plate fashioned like a fish.

Most of the 800 ceramic wares survived only in pieces, but Gonzales was able to discern the bones of llamas, deer, guinea pigs, and fish among the sherds, suggesting that the pottery had once contained food. Bottles may have originally held corn beer. Mixed in with the food refuse were 233 human bones belonging to 21 children, juveniles, and adults, which raises at least the possibility of ritual cannibalism; supporting studies that might confirm this hypothesis have yet to be reported, however.

As at ancient Garagay, hallucinogens played an integral role in Chavin de Huantar's ceremonies. In fact, according to Richard Burger, characteristics of the tenoned heads on the temple's perimeter walls reveal the four stages that a shaman undergoes while transforming from a human to either a supernatural jaguar, a bird of prey, or a hybrid of the pair. In the first stage, facial wrinkles suggest the onset of nausea, a common side effect of psychoactive drugs. In the second stage, the eyes begin to bulge, the expression becomes contorted, and mucus hangs from the nose. This, according to 17th-century Spanish traveler and chronicler Pedro Simón, was a sign—much coveted by Muisca Indians of his day—that the drug had begun to work its transformative magic. "They take these powders," the friar wrote, "and put them in their noses and which, because they are pungent, make the mucous flow until it hangs down into the mouth, which they observe in a mirror, and when it runs straight down it is a good sign."

Large fangs dominate the third-stage sculptures, whose features have grown markedly feline. By the fourth stage, the metamorphosis is complete: The shaman—half crested eagle, half cat—has become a flying jaguar, mediator between the natural and supernatural realms.

Six fish hammered out of sheet gold and dangling from a gold choker still bear traces of cinnabar, a red mineral that was used to bring out the design. Dating from the Chavin period, the 18-inch-long necklace was retrieved by graverobbers somewhere along the north coast of Peru.

According to Burger, the physiological reactions portrayed in these sculptures—wrinkles, nausea, bulging eyes, nasal discharge—imply that the drug partaken of by the shamans was some form of hallucinogenic snuff, probably the ground-up beans of the vilca tree or the pulverized leaves and bark of the epena tree. In addition, several foot-long stone mortars suitable for preparing such powders have been unearthed at Chavin de Huantar. Too small to have been used for grinding grain, they were exquisitely sculpted in the shape of jaguars and raptorial birds.

Use of the San Pedro cactus was also intimately tied to ritual practice at Chavin de Huantar. In the frieze embellishing the original temple's circular plaza, robed priests—one wearing an elaborate headdress with a dangling jaguar tail, another carrying a ribbed staff of San Pedro cactus—move in procession toward the central staircase. Jaguars with the taloned feet of eagles keep pace beneath them. Burger believes the frieze represents Chavin de Huantar's functionaries in their two complementary forms: temple priests presiding over public rituals and flying jaguars transmuted through the hallucinogenic medium of the San Pedro cactus.

The rites that were practiced at Chavin de Huantar had a power to inspire belief without precedent in the early history of Peru. Indeed, traces of Chavin de Huantar's far-ranging influence have been identified over a 77,000-square-mile area—a territory approximately the size of Portugal.

One of the largest caches of Chavinoid artifacts found to date was unearthed on the southern fringe of this culture-defined area, more than 325 miles distant in the seaside cemetery of Karwa, near Paracas. In 1970 huaqueros uncovered a large rectangular tomb containing the bodies of several individuals and over 200 fragments of brightly painted cloth. When painstakingly pieced together by North American archaeologist Alana Cordy-Collins, the fragments formed gargantuan banners, some measuring as much as nine feet high and 12 feet long. More important, each had been embellished with larger-than-life images drawn from Chavin de Huantar's pantheon: the Staff God, the great caiman, and their retinue of jaguars, serpents, and winged guardians.

All of the figures had been rendered in orthodox Chavin style using new textile paints in colors of blue, tan, brown, green, and red-

A fragment of a finely painted cotton textile discovered by looters at Karwa, near Paracas in the desert of Peru's southern coast, is covered with a pattern depicting the Staff God holding serpent-headed staffs in each hand—the inspiration for the name archaeologists have given him. That the deity was rendered in the Chavin style leads scholars to think that Karwa may have been a regional Chavin cult center.

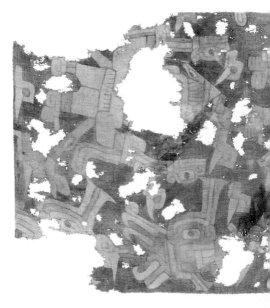

dish orange. Together with the banners' giant size, the decorations led Cordy-Collins to conclude that the panels, though too fragile to have existed out of doors for very long, may have adorned the walls of a local shrine or been paraded like standards through the streets on ceremonial occasions.

However these textiles were used, Richard Burger speculates that by the time of their production—around 390 BC—Karwa had itself become a secondary cult center. His conjecture is based on a small but significant change in the way Karwa artisans frequently depicted the Staff God: Normally—as configured on the Raimondi Stone as well as other pieces of Chavin monumental sculpture—the deity is represented as male. On the Karwa textiles, however, the image is portrayed as female. Moreover, in place of the usual serpentine headdress, the Karwa Staff Goddess sports a crown composed primarily of cotton balls.

For assistance in interpreting these variations, Burger turned to the model of the cult of Pachacamac. According to Spanish chroniclers, oracles existed all along the Peruvian coast to Pachacamac's north and south. These secondary cult centers were conceived of as branches—the wives, siblings, and children of the Pachacamac supernatural. Each oracle was granted its own origin myth and collection of local symbols.

Karwa, Burger suggests, may have been such a branch oracle. By extrapolation, the Karwa Staff Goddess might be seen as the wife, sister, or daughter of the great Staff God of Chavin de Huantar. Her

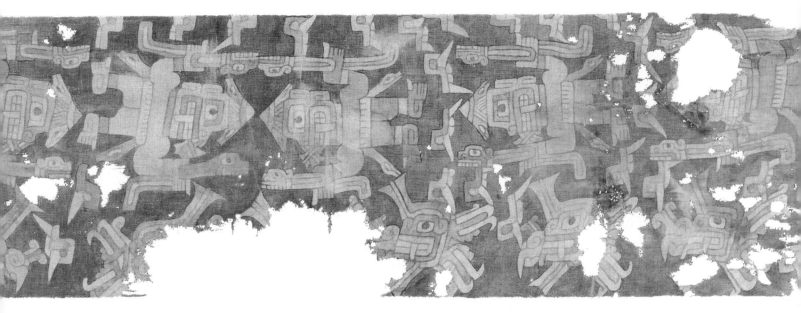

cotton headdress would identify her as the supernatural patroness of cotton, the coastal region's premier cultivated plant. In return for her protection and divine guidance, the peoples of Karwa and the surrounding region would have donated a substantial portion of their cotton yield to Chavin de Huantar as tribute.

Evidence for other secondary cult centers has so far eluded archaeologists. In the northern Lambayeque Valley not far from the coastal city of Chiclayo, however, workers constructing an airfield unearthed a remarkable conch-shell trumpet believed to have been used in Chavinoid rituals *(page 73)*. The shell's whorled tip had been cut off, and a hole had been drilled at the other end, perhaps to allow for a strap or cord. Its surface had been painstakingly incised with the figure of a supernatural blowing on a conch shell from which snakes and jaguarlike faces emanated like musical notes. Tello speculated that a Chavin officiant may have once worn the instrument around his neck and blown into the truncated apex to summon the gods or to invite their counsel.

Such artifacts, along with the beautiful and unusual Chavin ceramics, have excited archaeologists, but it is gold that bedazzles. According to Tello, in 1928 or 1929 a group of boys playing in an irrigation ditch located near the woman's grave at Chongoyape discovered a trove of gold Chavinoid objects whose splendor rivaled that of the woman's burial gifts. A 15-year-old named Floro Morrofú first spotted the treasures. After freeing them from the sandy soil, he distributed them among his friends, placing a tall crown on the head of one boy and a bracelet on another. Morrofú was drawing two enormous sheets of gold—presumably the remains of ceremonial vases—over his calves like leggings, when the owner of the property, attracted from afar by the gleam of the metal, appeared on horseback and tried to coax the boys into surrendering their spoils. Most turned tail and ran, grabbing what loot they could; a few surrendered their finds for a modest tip.

Among the pieces that remained or could later be gathered, archaeologists counted three crowns, a headdress, a pair of tweezers, and 10 earspools—all of gold. Judging by the tweezers, which are thought to have been used to pluck out beard hairs, and the heaviness of the earspools, North American archaeologist Samuel K. Lothrop proposed that the grave belonged to a prominent male. Each bore lavish Chavin designs: The image of a plumed jaguar surrounded by writhing serpents adorned the largest crown; an anthro-

A nine-and-a-half-inch-tall crown, made of beaten gold and embossed with the Chavin Staff God, is among the earliest surviving gold objects found in the Americas. From a tomb near the town of Chongoyape, in the Lambayeque Valley of northern Peru, the crown probably was worn by its owner on ceremonial occasions and then buried with him.

pomorphic jaguar holding a staff in each hand appeared on another.

Other isolated gold finds have been made throughout the Chavin-culture area. Most are simple, hammered sheets of gold, but a few are figures in the round. Among these, the showpiece is a five-inch-long gold snuff spoon that is believed to be one of the Andes' first three-dimensional metal objects to survive into modern times. Its handle bears the finely crafted image of a mythical figure blowing into a silver conch shell.

Though hammering was already a well-established Andean goldworking tradition, the techniques used to produce this and other exquisite goldworks *(pages 35-47)*—soldering and sweat welding among them—had no antecedents in the New World. Yet they would become the hallmark of the craft for the next thousand years. To North American archaeologist Heather Lechtman, their presence implies the existence of highly skilled smiths—who may even have been employed permanently at Chavin de Huantar.

The inventiveness that characterized the work of the Early Horizon goldsmiths was echoed in the creations of the period's textile artisans as well. For the first time, fabrics with a standardized loom width, about 13 inches, appeared, suggesting that they were products of an organized, group effort. The heddle loom came into use, incorporating a mechanical device that lifted and lowered the lengthwise warp yarns so the weaver could manually insert the crosswise fibers of the weft. And paints were applied directly to textiles to create such designs as those on the Karwa banners.

This burst of technological innovation, says Burger, can be attributed in large part to the Chavin cult itself, whose spread forged ideological links between distant communities and fostered an unparalleled exchange of goods and ideas. The advances also reflect the superlative efforts of Chavin artists to create awe-inspiring works by transcending the methods and materials of the time. Portable catechisms, these image-and-symbol-packed creations had been designed to communicate the cult's otherworldly message.

In the opinion of Lechtman, the sudden, widespread appearance of gold artifacts in the archaeological record of the Early Horizon probably expresses a certain "religious and ceremonial bias" of the cult for the metal. Dazzling to the eye and nearly incorruptible, gold became associated with notions of eternity and the sun, and hence with fertility and abundance. Like shamans, Chavin goldsmiths would have been seen as masters of their own kind of transforma-

Fashioned out of sheets of gold and silver, this snuff spoon shows a priestly figure blowing a ceremonial conch shell. Snuff, made apparently of strong tobacco as well as narcotic plants, was used in rituals.

tion—able, with the help of fire and a simple hammer, to change a lump of metal into a sacred object.

By and large, the sublime surviving gold wares and textiles of the Chavin cult seem to have been the exclusive property of a privileged few. A survey of these artifacts by Burger has revealed that most were discovered in elite burials and that most were objects of adornment or personal use. A kind of theocratic aristocracy—a select class of individuals who used their ties to the cult to legitimize their authority and to promote their personal wealth—accompanied the spread of Chavin, it appears. The woman buried at Chongoyape was doubtless such an individual.

The carvings on this 10-inch-long strombus, or conch shell, unearthed in the Lambayeque Valley, suggest that it may have been played as a trumpet in Chavin rituals. The incised image depicts a mystical being blowing a conch shell as snakes and jaguar heads stream from the opening.

Signs of this nascent social stratification can be read in the ruins of the community that once encircled Chavin de Huantar. Excavations conducted in the late 1970s by Burger indicate that, from a 15-acre settlement of some 500 farmers and herders in 850 BC, the village of Chavin de Huantar grew—over a period of some 600 years—to a city of 2,000 to 3,000 inhabitants scattered over a hundred-acre expanse. Large quantities of Spondylus shell fragments, the majority of which were by-products of bead and pendant production, litter one area of the ancient city. Their discovery may suggest that Chavin de Huantar's means to obtain the highly prized shells was greater than that of other communities, as items made from the imported shells were probably intended not only for local use, but also for exchange with visitors.

On the wide, well-built terraces surrounding the temple precinct, Burger uncovered the remains of houses with tall stone walls and niches. The residents, whose kitchen middens indicate they dined on the tender meat of young llamas, were undoubtedly Chavin de Huantar's economic elite. A bit of hammered gold found on the floor of one of these dwellings was probably once worn as a mark of rank. By contrast, most of Chavin de

Huantar's populace lived in a separate sector where Burger found neither luxury items nor the remains of fine foodstuffs, and only stone foundations of dwellings were uncovered.

Ironically, perhaps, it was humble folk who ultimately inherited the grand plazas and hallowed galleries of Chavin de Huantar. Inexplicably, sometime in the third century BC, the fabric of Chavin culture began to tear apart. Lacking the strong, centralized state apparatus that many scholars believe is required for a society to maintain long-term stability, the Chavin cult, it is thought, ultimately broke into rival communities that adopted clashing ideological and economic programs. Ceremonial centers throughout central and northern Peru were abandoned, and hilltop fortresses appeared in both coastal and highland valleys. At Chavin de Huantar, a rustic village grew up atop the circular plaza, and pieces of the temple's stone carvings were incorporated into the walls of peasant huts. The subterranean galleries and canals, no longer assiduously maintained, became choked with mud, and sacred galleries were gradually transformed into mausoleums.

Not surprisingly, the pottery that helps scholars mark the spread of the Chavin culture now vanishes from the archaeological record. But neither the artistic traditions nor the fearsome gods and mythical beasts that once inspired them would be forgotten. Indeed, 1,800 years after the priests of Chavin de Huantar had ceased celebrating their liturgy, the Spanish chronicler Antonio Vásquez de Espinoza visited the site and found that it retained a powerful mystique.

Writing in 1617, he described a "large building of huge stone blocks very well wrought; it was one of the most famous of the heathen sanctuaries, like Rome or Jerusalem with us; the Indians used to come and make their offerings and sacrifices, for the Devil pronounced many oracles from here, and so they repaired here from all over the kingdom."

CONTACTING THE SPIRITS

Among the pre-Columbian relics discovered by archaeologists and graverobbers alike have been numerous curiosities—many of them exquisitely wrought in gold—associated with shamanism and the world of the spirits. Thanks to contemporary ethnographic studies of shamans, the accounts of various Spanish chroniclers at the time of the conquest (some writing out of prejudice, others out of genuine interest), and the archaeological record, light has been shed on the use and meaning of these fascinating objects. Taken together, all bear out the deeply held Indian belief that sickness and death resulted from interference by the supernatural. Thus the practice of shamanism by astute and insightful members of various Central and South American societies was (and remains) an attempt to mediate between the seen and the unseen worlds, between humans and the multiple forces that influence their lives.

By consuming consciousness-enhancing narcotics, the shaman of old strove to preserve the moral and social order of his community, acquire cures for diseases, foretell the future, and ward off evil magic. He also divined how and when his people should hunt, fish, and plant crops. The shaman's motives could be dark at times: He might travel to the spirit world to inflict illness on a personal enemy. But in everything, he sought the benefaction of his supernatural masters.

The Muisca-style figure above, made of a gold-and-copper alloy, sits in a ritual squatting position that is often associated with shamanic practices and ceremonies. Far from relaxing, a shaman in such a pose was in a state of intense concentration, focusing on internal sensations or on external stimuli—such as the flickering lights of a live ember or the color spectrum of rock crystals, perhaps to the accompaniment of sacred chants or the rhythmic beat of a gourd rattle. Under such conditions, in the words of a present-day shaman, "the horizon opens up like a door."

PATHWAY TO THE SUPERNATURAL

To establish contact with the spirit world, the shamans turned—and still do—to the divine powers supposedly resident in certain hallucinogenic plant preparations. The organic chemical constituents in these substances act on the central nervous system to trigger visions of a wide range of images—often brilliant colors in kaleidoscopic motion—as well as auditory, tactile, and olfactory sensations. The trance state that results became the shaman's personal pathway to the supernatural, an ecstatic bridge across which lay realms hidden from ordinary mortals.

Of all the plants used by Andean peoples in the past as well as today, the most common, as well as the most revered, is coca, which is found all over the region and is frequently represented in its ancient art. By chewing the leaves of this stimulant along with lime obtained from seashells that have been burned and ground, Indians achieve a euphoric effect that they consider to be an expression of the plant's spiritual energy. No ancient shaman dared draw near the supernatural without first ritually chewing on some coca, releasing the inherent power of the leaf.

Decorative figures crown the gold spatulas below, and a sculpted naked woman stands guard over the gold narrow-necked flask, or poporo, *at left, all part of the drug paraphernalia of pre-Hispanic Colombia. An Indian would wet the end of a spatula, use it to draw a small amount of powdered lime from the flask, and place the lime in the mouth next to a wad of masticated coca leaves. The lime acted as a catalyst to free the cocaine from the plant.*

Typical of the flat, wedge-shaped *tunjos* of the Muisca is this male figure, who helps himself to some lime with a spatula. Mostly fashioned of alloys of copper and gold, such votive objects were interred at burial sites or cast into mountain lakes as offerings to the gods.

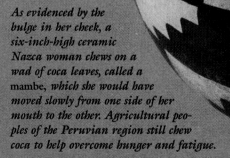

As evidenced by the bulge in her cheek, a six-inch-high ceramic Nazca woman chews on a wad of coca leaves, called a *mambe*, which she would have moved slowly from one side of her mouth to the other. Agricultural peoples of the Peruvian region still chew coca to help overcome hunger and fatigue.

Shamans eager to peer into the spirit world have turned to hundreds of different plants, many of them more powerful than coca and all regarded as sacred. For Central and South America are particularly rich in psychotropic flora, and over the centuries their peoples have discovered a whole range of flora that induce ritual intoxication, learning to combine one species with another to manipulate the intensity of the ecstatic experience. They have smoked strong tobacco, inhaled vision-inducing snuff, and imbibed a liquid made from the tall San Pedro cactus.

The mescaline-bearing San Pedro has been depicted in ceremonial art for at least 3,000 years. Widely used at the time of the European conquest, this most potent hallucinogen—which can cause those who take it to "hear" colors and "see" sounds—is still much sought after by present-day Peruvian folk healers, particularly the rare four-ribbed variety (*right*), which is considered to have special curative powers. Traditionally, the cactus is cut into slices and boiled for several hours, often with the addition of other ingredients. The resulting brew is either drunk or poured into the nostrils. Today some doctors use mescaline in psychotherapy to get at their patients' childhood memories.

Perhaps recalling the ecstatic state of a shaman, a trancelike look of contentment covers the face atop a gold pendant from the Quimbaya region of Colombia. By concentrating on the small, mobile plaques of such jingly ornaments, shamans could enhance the effects of intoxicants; they also believed that the glitter of the gold transmitted its energy to the looker.

A fanged and clawed supernatural being with serpentine hair clutches a four-ribbed San Pedro cactus in this carved stone relief from Chavin de Huantar, in the northern highlands of Peru. Archaeologists have dated the carving to around 1300 BC, making it the earliest known representation of the sacred cactus.

A ubiquitous motif in South American mythology and art, the elegant little gold amphibian at right from Colombia may represent the Bufo marinus toad, whose skin glands contain the potent alkaloid bufotenine, a hallucinogen. Indians from Amazonian Peru still introduce the dangerous toxic directly into the bloodstream by rubbing it on self-inflicted cuts.

FLYING HIGH ON THE WINGS OF DRUGS

According to the cosmovision of Andean shamans still practicing today, the universe is made up of a series of echeloned worlds—as many as nine, according to one contemporary Colombian tribe. It is by gaining access to the part of the universe beyond the everyday world that the shaman is thought to glean insights into areas closed to other, less spiritually endowed, humans. To penetrate these realms, the shaman undergoes metamorphosis; in a state of drug-induced euphoria, he leaves the temporal world, convinced that he has been transformed into a bird.

During his magical journey into other dimensions of consciousness, the shaman imagines himself flying above unknown territory to reach remote regions of the universe, where he acquires much of his esoteric knowledge. As the soaring voyage of the soul ends, the shaman falls back to earth, his mission over. Modern scholars have brought a pharmacological eye to this shamanic flight, noting that a commonly experienced psychic effect of many hallucinogens is levitation, the out-of-body sensation of gliding through the air and visiting distant places. The herbal ointments concocted by the witches of medieval Europe produced similar perceptions of flight.

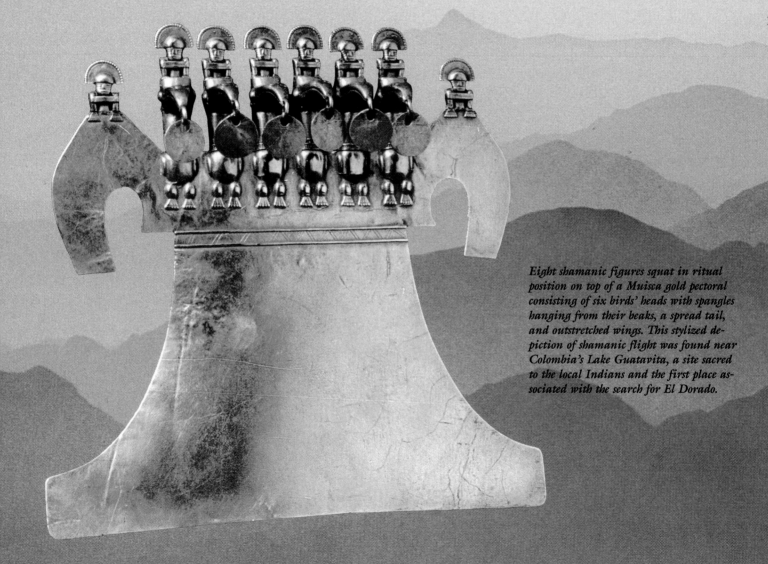

Eight shamanic figures squat in ritual position on top of a Muisca gold pectoral consisting of six birds' heads with spangles hanging from their beaks, a spread tail, and outstretched wings. This stylized depiction of shamanic flight was found near Colombia's Lake Guatavita, a site sacred to the local Indians and the first place associated with the search for El Dorado.

Back arched and head thrown back, an ecstatic shaman carrying a striped baton and feathered fan appears to soar through the air in this detail from a Paracas textile. Since a bird's capacity for flight resides in its wing feathers, a fan like the one above, charged with supernatural power, may have been used in ceremonies to bestow symbolically on the shaman the ability to fly. The 2,000-year-old fan was recovered from a grave on the arid Paracas Peninsula in the 1920s.

81

TAKING ON THE TRAITS OF THE JAGUAR

In their quest for the supernatural, shamans connect with many creatures. Of particular significance are animals that alter their appearance by shedding their skins and shells, like snakes and crabs, and those that undergo metamorphosis, like butterflies. And the hummingbird, often depicted in pre-Columbian art, is said to represent the shaman's ability to suck pathogens from victims of witchcraft. The spotted jaguar, however, is the animal most closely associated with the shaman.

A solitary nocturnal hunter, this most powerful of South American predators regularly crosses from one realm to another—from night to day—echoing the shaman's movement between celestial spheres. Indeed, so close is the bond between jaguar and shaman that some tribes use the same word, derived from the term for cohabitation, for both. The nature of the beast's power is ambivalent, however: While the jaguar spirit may be a helper and protector, used for beneficial ends, it can also be an aggressive force that threatens or kills. It is up to the shaman, whose own duality embodies both society and nature, to use this power for good, to channel the vital energy and tame the jaguar within.

The squat, snarling jaguar-man at left is one of dozens that dot the hillsides around San Agustín in Colombia's Magdalena River valley. Despite its prominent feline fangs, broad, flat nose, and almond-shaped eyes, the stone statue depicts a man only partly turned into a jaguar; the hands, legs, and body are all human.

A jaguar overpowering a naked victim has been carved into this seven-inch finial, which adorned a large Moche wooden staff. Some Indians still believe that all jaguars that attack humans are shamans in animal form, and that when shamans die they turn into the beasts permanently.

The fanged figure in distinctive Moche headdress on this 12-inch-high spouted jar makes supplication to guardian spirits that reputedly lived high in the Andes. A woman in a checkered cloak and carrying a bundle on her back huddles across from a bound prisoner who awaits probable execution; such sacrifices—by tossing the unfortunate down onto the rocks below—were made in the hope that the mountain-dwelling spirits would send rain.

THE MOCHE:
A PEOPLE RAISED
FROM THE GRAVE

A smile brings a 1,500-year-old clay bottle to life, an example of the Moche potters' penchant for realism. The stirrup-like protuberance is the vessel's handle and spout.

As the Roman Empire was reaching its fullness after the first century AD, a surprising and mysterious people was developing its own remarkable civilization along the north coast of Peru. Lacking a written language, the Americans left no texts to help scholars understand their culture. Indeed, the name by which they are now known—Moche—derives not from some aged inscription, but from the name of the modern village of Moche near the Huaca de la Luna, or the Pyramid of the Moon, one of a pair of ceremonial structures this group erected east of Trujillo. Yet throughout the arid 340-mile-long, 50-mile-wide strip of coastland that from AD 100 to 800 was the Moche realm, archaeologists have uncovered ample evidence of past greatness.

To harness the rivers that flow down the Andes to the Pacific, for instance, the Moche constructed ingenious irrigation canals that dramatically increased the land available to them for cultivation. Moche farmers were tilling as many as 100,000 acres in the Jequetepeque Valley alone—an amount greater than that worked by Peruvian farmers as late as the 1960s. To obtain lapis lazuli, red-edged spondylus shells, brightly colored feathers, and other valuable raw materials, the Moche plied trade networks that reached as far north as Ecuador and as far south as Chile. And to express themselves and their spiritual lives, they built enormous pyramids, palaces, and temples out of millions of sun-dried mud bricks and crafted unique ceramics and gleaming gold, gilded copper, and silver ornaments. Of these, the clay objects—such as the lifelike stirrup-spout bottle on page 84 and others shown on pages 113-121—provide scholars with their most absorbing picture of the Moche.

For more than 20 years, Christopher B. Donnan, director of the Fowler Museum of Cultural History at the University of California, Los Angeles, has overseen the creation of a huge photographic archive of such pottery and other Moche artwork. The repository, which is maintained at UCLA and contains more than 135,000 photographs of artifacts held in museums and private collections throughout the world, serves as a kind of visual database that archaeologists can consult while attempting to interpret the results of their fieldwork in Peru.

Ceramics constitute the majority of pictures in the archive. Realistically modeled and painted, the works show the Moche en-

Offering a detailed look at Moche ceremonial life, this scene copied from a ceramic bottle depicts human sacrifice. In the lower panel bound prisoners are having their throats cut; in the upper panel, figures carry vessels that contain the victims' blood. The short figure, third from right in the top row (C), is a priestess, behind whom stands an attendant (D). Despite the solemnity of the occasion, a begging dog rears on its haunches between the so-called Warrior Priest (A) and Bird Priest (B), seen facing each other.

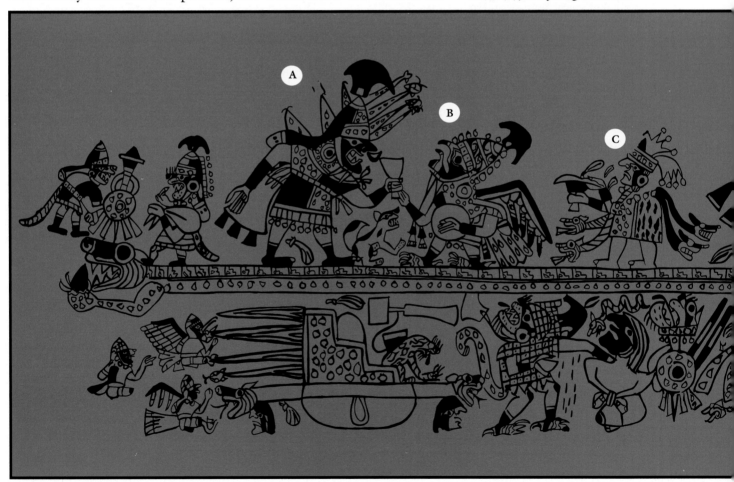

gaging in such seemingly mundane activities as hunting, fishing, making music, having sex, and triumphantly tugging the hair of vanquished enemies. Creatures such as sea lions, deer, and monkeys are lovingly rendered as well, as are architectural features, such as small square houses. Here, evidently, is a photographic montage of life as lived by the Moche.

Yet the more Donnan studied his collection of Moche images, the more he wondered about what was missing from them. "I began to realize," he wrote in 1990, "that many everyday activities, such as farming, cooking, and pottery making, are never shown. We see nobody laying up mud bricks, thatching a roof, or making a wattle-and-daub wall. Why are everyday activities such as these ignored?" The answer, he believed, was that Moche artists were not depicting simple daily activities even when it seemed that they were. Rather, they selected only particular tasks that had ceremonial or religious meaning for them. "I now realize," Donnan wrote, "that art expresses the religious and supernatural aspects of Moche culture and that virtually nothing of everyday life is illustrated for its own sake."

This special nature of Moche art is dramatically depicted in what has come to be known as the sacrifice ceremony. In it, four splendidly dressed Moche personages—identified by Donnan as figures A, B, C, and D—preside over the death of bound prisoners of war and then collect their blood in goblets for ritual consumption. The practice, or the belief in it, seems to have been widespread: Artifacts looted by graverobbers in the 1960s in the northernmost reaches of the Moche kingdom, at Loma Negra, near Peru's present-day border with Ecuador, bore sacrifice-ceremony iconography. Likewise, a mural painted on the walls of a ceremonial center unearthed in the late 1940s at Pañamarca, 300 miles to the south in the Nepeña Valley, displays both bound prisoners and ceremonially dressed figures who hold tall cups with pedestal bases. Although the scenes vary slightly in their details, the participants and key elements remain the same for all.

Thanks to Donnan's archive at UCLA, researchers know the roles played by the four participants. Figure A, a large, imposing man of fearsome mien, has been named the Warrior Priest. Included in every representation of the sacrifice ceremony, he wears a conical helmet topped with a crescent-shaped decoration, prominent ear and nose ornaments, and a back flap, a bladelike piece of protective armor that dangled from the belts of Moche warriors. Symbolic, perhaps, of the Warrior Priest's exalted position, rays emanate from his head and shoulders, and he is often depicted carrying a scepter with a boxlike chamber at one end.

Figure B offers a blood-filled goblet to the Warrior Priest. He wears either a conical helmet or, more often, a headdress with an owl at its center. For this reason, scholars refer to him as the Bird Priest. Figure C, who was identified as a priestess, also holds a goblet and is frequently pictured standing near a large basin that contains a number of drinking vessels. Clad in a dresslike garment and a headpiece featuring stylized plumes with serrated ends, she wears her hair in long braids that hang down to her feet and terminate in serpent heads. The final figure, D, wears a sash and a headdress with an animal face and long streamers.

The capture and public display of prisoners—events portrayed on countless ceramic pieces in the UCLA archive—are regarded as important facets of Moche society. But lacking convincing archaeological evidence that the sacrifice ceremony portrayed at Loma Negra, Pañamarca, and elsewhere had actually taken place, Donnan had long suspected it was mythical. Then, in 1987 and again in 1991, he came across startling proof that the scenes of celebration and gore depicted actual rites.

Donnan and Peruvian archaeologist Luis Jaime Castillo made the more recent discovery while excavating three Moche tombs at San José de Moro in the lower Jequetepeque Valley. The chambers, which all dated to approximately AD 700, had much in common: Each had been fashioned from mud bricks and roofed with wooden beams, which were by now disintegrated, and crammed with an array of ceramic vessels, cups, ceremonial knives, masks, and jewelry. Each tomb's principal occupant had been laid faceup, and the remains of llamas or human companions were discovered nearby. But one tomb was more elaborate than the others. Its walls contained special niches that were filled with ceramic vessels and parts of sacrificed llamas, and on the floor lay artifacts that had to have been obtained hundreds of miles away. Ecuadoran spondylus shells rested upon the chest and hands of the occupant, a woman, and beads of Chilean lapis lazuli lay near her neck.

Hammered metal arms and legs covered her moldered limbs, and a mask was found near her skull. Made of a silver-copper alloy, these items, together with the shells and beads, supported the impression that the woman had enjoyed high status during her lifetime.

Oxidized silver hands rising above her skull in a horrifying image of death, a Moche priestess still wears the shell-and-lapis-lazuli necklace with which she was buried. Her tomb at San José de Moro in Peru's lower Jequetepeque Valley, among the richest Moche female graves ever uncovered and studied scientifically, dates from around AD 700. Found with her were a silver ornamental headdress, similar to one worn by priestesses depicted on Moche pottery, and a large ceramic basin with goblet and cups inside resembling those used in ceremonies involving human sacrifices. These vessels suggest her role in bloodletting rituals.

But what seized Donnan's attention were two huge, bow-shaped silver plumes with zigzag ends discovered lying near her head and a large black-ware ceramic basin that had been placed in a corner of the tomb. The plumes once were part of an elaborate headdress now rotted away. The basin contained three squat cups and one tall goblet that had been painted with decorative swirls and images of anthropomorphic beings drinking from similar vessels.

For Donnan, the discovery was like meeting the original subject of an often seen photograph. At once he realized that the occupant of the tomb was a priestess, the priestess of the sacrifice ceremony—Figure C of the pots and the Pañamarca mural. He would have known her anywhere. Anything but mythical, as he had believed, she was real, one of a long series of priests and priestesses who played unchanging roles in a tightly scripted ritual and, conforming to tradition, apparently used the same kind of paraphernalia throughout the Moche realm. Their bloody ceremony, Donnan surmised, was no occasional event—it constituted an integral part of a state religion. When the participants passed away, they were buried with their ritual objects, and others of their class succeeded them in their role as keepers of the time-honored ceremony.

Donnan's remarkable breakthrough is all the more noteworthy considering that up until the verge of the 20th century, there had been no scientific examination of the Moche whatsoever. All that was known of the culture had been gleaned from the chronicles of European conquerors who arrived in South America some seven centuries after the culture's demise. Based on oral history, the accounts are anything but reliable sources for scientific inquiry, yet a few provide valuable hints about the Moche past.

    The author of one such chronicle, for instance, the Spanish missionary and historian Bartolomé de las Casas, addressed what even today are the most arresting monuments to the Moche civilization. "The lords of the shore-country," he wrote around 1550, "were wont to build their palaces upon the summits of hills or, if no suitable hill were available, they would cause their people to pile up vast amounts of earth so as to make an artificial eminence."

    To the unknowing traveler's eye, these eminences—hundreds of large platform-topped pyramids, or huacas, built not of piled-up earth but of dried mud bricks—can appear to have erupted like huge volcanic outcroppings in the fields and valleys and on the lower mountain slopes. One of them, the Huaca del Sol, or Pyramid of the Sun—in its time the greatest edifice in South America—still guards the coastal plain near present-day Trujillo. Now shrunken to a height of 135 feet by centuries of natural erosion and human mischief, the edifice once towered over 160 feet high, contained more than 143 million bricks, and covered more than 12.5 acres—making it a close equivalent in size to Egypt's Great Pyramid at Giza.

    Rumors that riches lay hidden within the huaca inevitably attracted the gold-seeking Spanish invaders. In 1532 they formed a company, sold stock to investors, and diverted a nearby river to wash away one side of the structure. The enterprise is thought to have netted great quantities of gold objects, though no records survive to describe how many pieces were actually found. All were probably melted down for bullion and lost forever. The Spaniards did, however, unwittingly perform one small service for the science of archaeology: In baring a cross section of the pyramid, they revealed that it had been enlarged and built upon many times throughout the centuries.

Only a third of its original size, the much eroded and looter-damaged Pyramid of the Sun still stands 135 feet high in the valley of the Moche River. It was assembled in eight stages from more than 143 million molded mud bricks that were set in clay mortar. The largest solid adobe structure in the New World, occupying more than 12.5 acres, it was painted red and other bright colors to render it an even more commanding sight.

The North American archaeologist Christopher Donnan kneels as he dusts off a partially buried Moche bottle in the shape of an owl during the 1989 excavation of a royal tomb at La Mina on Peru's northern coast. All told, six fine ceramic bottles, overlooked by grave-robbers, surfaced. The owl is a frequent subject of Moche art.

More than 300 years later, a German archaeologist named Max Uhle became the first man of science to investigate the Moche. Sponsored by the mother of wealthy newspaper publisher William Randolph Hearst, in 1899 he excavated 31 burials in the vicinity of the Huaca del Sol, the nearby Huaca de la Luna, and Moche, the present-day village that lent its name to the ancient culture. The objects Uhle unearthed and cataloged are housed today in the Phoebe Apperson Hearst Museum of Anthropology at the University of California, Berkeley, and remain one of the finest Moche research collections in the world.

A wealthy Peruvian sugar planter named Rafael Larco Hoyle followed in Uhle's footsteps in the 1930s and 1940s. Through purchases from private antiquities collectors and his own excavations, Larco amassed some 40,000 Moche ceramic pieces and thousands of textile fragments and metal and wood objects. A student of Moche iconography, he compared the artifacts with the age-old cultural traditions practiced by his fellow Peruvians and with clues hidden in early Spanish documents, and offered the archaeological world its first systematic reconstruction of Moche culture. His legacy is the Rafael Larco Herrera Museum in Lima, named in honor of his father.

Modern archaeologists have added much to Larco's reconstruction in recent decades. While exploring the valleys that crisscross the north coast of Peru, they have excavated more than 350 graves and identified scores of settlements. From these, scholars have been able to piece together not only the dwelling patterns and burial practices of the Moche, but also their eating habits. Investigators have found remnants of peanuts, corn, coca, beans, squash, manioc (cassava), chili peppers, pumpkins, cherimoya (a squash), and a member of the papaya family called the ulluchu that is thought to have anticoagulant properties necessary in such rites as the sacrifice ceremony, in which the blood of victims was drunk. Archaeologists have also turned up the bones of guinea pigs, llamas, ducks, fish, and sea lions and the remains of shellfish.

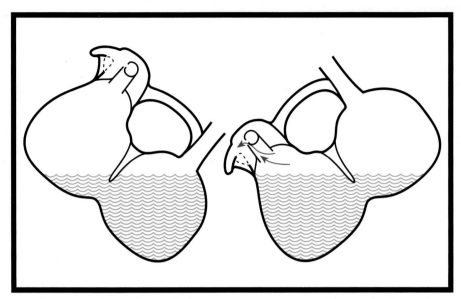

This Moche ceramic is a double-chambered whistling bottle. When partially filled with water through the spout and moved back and forth, it emits a warblelike whistle. The mechanism by which this happens is diagramed here. When the bottle is tilted backward, liquid fills the chamber directly under the spout. As the bottle is tilted the other way, the air that collected in the second chamber is forced through a tube attached to a hollow sphere and passes over a hole in the sphere to produce the sound. Whistling bottles, which may have had ceremonial uses, were made as early as 1000 BC in Peru and show up in 2,000 years of the archaeological record.

Documents from a later but not dissimilar age suggest that favorite foods were also favorite offerings. In 1585 the Jesuit priest Pablo Joseph de Arriaga arrived to devote himself to missionary life. Some 35 years later, back home in Madrid, he published a book in which he lamented what he considered the superstitions of the local inhabitants.

The principal offering, according to Father Pablo Joseph, was chicha, or corn beer. "It is a common saying with them that when they go to worship the huacas they are giving them a drink," he wrote of the Indians. "After they have poured it over the huaca to the extent they deem proper, the sorcerers drink the rest and it makes them act as if mad." Coca, from which cocaine is derived today, was another common offering. In fact, Indians in the area of the river Huamanmayu, located in the highlands 70 miles east of San José de Moro, cultivated no fewer than 14 coca fields belonging to the local huacas. "These fields," he noted, "we ordered to be burned."

His comments about other sacrifices cast a revealing light both on the animal bones found in Moche refuse and on the remains of llamas that accompanied the priestess at San José de Moro to the grave: "The llama . . . is also sacrificed during the most solemn festivals of the huacas," Father Pablo Joseph wrote. "They cut open his left side, take out the heart, and eat it raw by the mouthful. They sprinkle the huaca with blood and divide the meat among the ministers, giving some also to the rest of the Indians. In some places they raise young llamas especially for the huacas."

Given the great practical value placed on the animals throughout the Andes—they were prized as pack animals, as a source of meat and of dung, which was burned as fuel, and for their wool and hides—it is hardly surprising that llamas made meaningful sacrificial offerings as well or that the Moche included them among the many items that were interred with members of their culture's elite, such as the priestess. Two other participants in the blood sacrifice ceremony are known to have been interred with llamas as well. Their final resting place, which was not systematically located by scholars but stumbled upon by graverobbers, contained what Christopher Donnan would later characterize in print as the "richest treasures ever excavated archaeologically in the Western Hemisphere."

An ancient weaving technique still employed by some Peruvian Indian women today is delineated on the flared rim of this Moche bowl. Here, the weavers use backstrap looms. One end of each loom is tied to a tall wooden support, the other to a belt around the waist. By leaning backward, the women can control the tension of the vertical threads as they run yarn-wound spindles between them. Other spindles lie at the ready on the ground. The weavers are probably producing intricately patterned headbands.

Around midnight on February 16, 1987, Walter Alva, the director of the Brüning Archaeological Museum in Lambayeque and a colleague of Christopher Donnan, received a call from the police. *Huaqueros* digging into the smallest of three pyramids *(pages 98-99)* near the village of Sipán, a 45-minute drive southeast of Lambayeque, had apparently happened upon a tomb filled with extraordinary treasure. The haul was so rich, the police said, that the looters at once fell out, coming to blows over how the goods should be divided. The group then broke up, and one of its members—disgruntled because he felt he had been cheated out of his fair share—went to the police and spilled the story, including the identity of his accomplices.

Responsible for safeguarding such archaeological monuments

as the pyramids, the officials sped to Sipán at once and raided the home of some brothers who were alleged to be ringleaders. Much of the loot had already made its way onto the black market, but the police were able to seize what remained and to pull in two suspects for interrogation. Then they invited Alva to examine the spoils.

For years he had worked with the police in a usually vain effort to prevent graverobbing, and the police routinely turned over to him whatever looted objects they confiscated. As a result, Alva knew as much about the tombs of Sipán as anyone alive; he was familiar with the work of the huaqueros and the remnants—typically picked-over ceramic ware, stone or shell beads, and copper objects—they discarded. As he later told *National Geographic,* "What awaited me at the police station in February 1987, I was sure, would be but the poorest castoffs of a graverobber."

But when he laid eyes on the artifacts, he was stunned. A quick count of the pieces came to 33. A mere sample of the total looted from the tomb, they included circular ear ornaments almost four inches in diameter; an oval nose decoration made of gold; a semicircular gilded copper bell like those seen hanging from warriors' belts in Moche art; a number of small gold and gilded copper disks, spheres, and cones; and a collection of beads.

Two of the beads, made of gilded copper and measuring about six inches in diameter, had jaguarlike faces with eyes and fangs of shell. Four others were in the shape of peanuts, wrinkled and patterned exactly like those once harvested in the region. The most magnificent bead, however, was almost five inches tall and made of nearly pure gold; it gleamed as if it had been burnished only moments ago. Shaped like a human head, it featured big ears, an open mouth, and silver eyes *(page 101).*

Donnan, who arrived in Lambayeque to view the artifacts a short time later, was also amazed. "It was as though we had overnight doubled the amount of Moche gold that was known in all the collections in the world," he said. "The quality of the craftsmanship, of the metalworking and lapidary work surpassed anything we had ever seen before."

Meanwhile, the saga of the thieves continued. Police paid an unexpected call on another of the alleged looters. He was not at home, but behind his house lay dozens of smashed gilded copper ornaments and figurines. The objects had corroded to a pale green color over the centuries, obscuring the thin layer of gold that made them once gleam bright yellow. Apparently, the huaquero who claimed the pieces had judged them to be of no value on the black market, so he deliberately broke them and threw them away. Yet another police raid caught the graverobbers at home and on the defensive. Shots were fired, and one of the suspects was fatally wounded.

The events contributed to a mounting sense of alarm that tempered Alva's excitement over the confiscated artifacts. He knew that word of such finds spreads quickly: Huaqueros would soon be swarming over the pyramids in search of leftovers. Alva had to locate and secure the newly looted tomb before the stampede began, not simply to dredge up overlooked pieces but to learn as much as possible about the burial's original condition before it was destroyed.

Back at Sipán, Alva and the police discovered men, women, and children already scrabbling through the back dirt of the dig with colanders, sieves, pieces of window screen, and their bare hands. Some clutched gilded copper disks and turquoise beads, and a lucky few had even come up with small gold objects. It took hours for the police to disperse the crowd.

"The situation was quite dramatic and very complicated," he said later, "because most of the people were willing to destroy the monument. If we hadn't intervened, the destruction would have been complete—the way it's been at other archaeological sites. We had to persuade the people to stop what they were doing and have the police physically remove them."

Alva quickly surveyed the scene and was shocked by the devastation. "I remember my first visit to the site and how sick I felt," he recalled later, "as I looked at the destruction of what had once been a sacred place for the Moche." Before him yawned little more than a gutted hole in the ground.

Knowing it was only a matter of time before the looters came back, Alva sent for a small team—spearheaded by Peruvian archaeologists Susana Meneses and Luis Chero Zurita and including archaeology students from the National University of Trujillo—set up camp, and worked out a three-hour watch schedule to keep the platform clear of unwanted visitors round the clock. When a team member was not on duty, Alva arranged for one of four armed guards to take his or her place—and with good reason. "Several times," he wrote, "staccato bursts from the policeman's submachine gun shocked me from sleep—warning shots fired above the heads of huaqueros sneaking up in the dark."

READING THE IMAGES ON MOCHE POTS

Scenes painted on Moche pots contain a wealth of information, but they are difficult to photograph and read whole because of the pots' curves. Donna McClelland and Christopher Donnan of the University of California have come up with a method of flattening out scenes so they can be studied and compared with others similarly recorded.

Typically, Donnan will repeatedly photograph a pot from the same distance, rotating and tilting it until all of its details have been captured *(below)*. Then McClelland creates drawings by placing each shot in sequence under tracing paper and

copying the outlines. She concentrates on only the central images to avoid distortion and takes pains to work out spatial relationships. Next, she uses her drawings to duplicate the scene on clear acetate, placing the photographs underneath in the positions indicated by her drawings and tracing the lines with a pen *(below)*. The finished work is called a roll-out and offers a two-dimensional look at the images covering a three-dimensional pot.

The protection allowed Alva to concentrate on two important tasks: clearing out the dirt and debris left by the huaqueros and the villagers, and mapping the overall structure of the three pyramids, including especially the one that housed the looted tomb. Workers using tall ladders, buckets, and ropes spent days on the first chore, and the pit steadily grew deeper until, 23 feet down, the diggers found themselves in a gaping hole that branched into a labyrinth of caverns and tunnels. The passageways, which had been dug by graverobbers, stood as monuments to frustration, as each one led not to a tomb of riches but to a wall of dirt.

Team members assigned to the second task discovered subtle differences in the composition, color, size, and shape of the bricks from which the smallest pyramid was made, along with variations in the mortar that held them together. From this, Meneses surmised that the monument had probably been constructed during the first century AD and then enlarged at least five times, the last expansion having been completed about AD 300. So many bricks were used that Alva assumed hundreds of workers must have been involved in each construction phase—either making and drying the bricks, passing them in relays to the building site, or actually setting them in place.

Individual marks on the blocks led the archaeologist to speculate that several labor forces, each from a different community and assigned a specific section of the site, might have been at work at any time. Every group, it is thought, sought to distinguish its work from that of the others, so the brickmakers scratched *Xs*, tridents, circles, and other identifying symbols on the bricks before they dried. Some workers, Alva found, even left impressions of their fingers or hands. "I find it eerie," he wrote, "to splay my hand across such a brick and find my fingers perfectly matched to those of another, long dead."

It was thus with a sense of recognition and excitement that the team scraping the bottom of the huaqueros' pit discovered bricks showing equally revealing but quite different marks: the imprints of long-disintegrated wooden beams that had once formed the ceiling of a small chamber. The bricks had been laid before sockets for support posts had been cut and later than the surrounding blocks in that part of the pyramid, indicating that the room had not been part of

Once-grand pyramids of Sipán rise heavily eroded from their bases in Peru's Lambayeque River valley. The small, flat-topped mound visible in the foreground contained a number of tombs, including that of the Warrior Priest. The larger structures still await excavation—their treasures yet unknown.

the structure's original construction. Alva concluded that it had been specially carved sometime around AD 300 to bury a Moche ruler.

To the archaeologists' delight, more than just dirt and destruction waited in the chamber. When they cleared the debris along one of its sides they found a number of unexpected treasures: a gilded copper object over six inches tall that Alva took to be a remnant of a broken crown; four ceramic jars that had been modeled into the form of human figures, one of whom stood almost eight and a half inches high and clutched a club in one hand and a shield in the other; and—yet more exciting—a life-size copper mask depicting a human face with eyes of inlaid turquoise. Nearby the archaeologists unearthed two gilded copper beads in the shape of owl heads, each less than two inches in diameter, and a pair of gilded copper ear ornaments that resembled those confiscated by the police.

Silver eyes set with lapis lazuli irises, this gold five-inch-high bead was stolen from the Moche platform mound at Sipán and recovered by police. Its twin was reportedly offered for $60,000 in the illegal antiquities market.

Seen from the air, the destruction wrought by graverobbers craters a Moche cemetery. The looting is done by unemployed laborers who sell their finds to unethical antiquities dealers as a way of supplementing their income from seasonal work.

Next came an even more impressive and surprising find—a copper scepter, apparently overlooked by the huaqueros because it had been embedded in the tomb's sidewall. More than three feet long and heavy, the staff was topped by a structure that looked like a dais with a peaked roof for a canopy. On the dais a woman copulated with a fantastic creature, half feline and half reptile, and along the ridgeline of the roof were 17 minuscule, double-faced, helmeted human heads. Surely, Alva thought, the scepter had been an important ceremonial object, the emblem of an exceedingly high-ranking figure in Moche society.

Further searching revealed that the huaqueros had left nothing else in the burial chamber, so Alva turned his attention to the summit of the pyramid, where he prepared to sink a shaft straight through the monument's core. He had his team mark off an area 10 meters square, which he then subdivided into 100 units, each of which measured one meter, or a little more than a yard, on a side. Only after recording every surface feature within the grid did the archaeologists set to work probing selected squares.

In a unit near the northwest corner of the excavation area, the diggers came across a section of the platform where, centuries before, the bricks had been removed and replaced with a fill of small stones and sand. Alva and Chero were struck by the notion that the fill, though old, was not as old as the surrounding brick. Anxiously clearing the fill, they exposed the powdered remains of eight decomposed wood beams, which were found to have once covered a rectangular chamber about nine and a half feet long, almost six feet wide, and a little over four feet deep. Using soft paintbrushes to brush away the dirt, they began the tedious task of exposing the chamber's contents.

"At last," Alva wrote, "the flick of a brush bared the lid of a red clay pot, and tedium vanished. Now every fillip exposed small pots, bowls, beakers, jars." Before the archaeologists lay pottery for different needs: utilitarian ware for household cooking and storage, quantities of red-clay beakers so nearly identical that they must surely have been mass-produced in molds; and beautifully crafted vessels decorated with portraits, plants, and animals; scenes depicting burials, women giving birth, prisoners being tortured, musicians playing their instruments. The total came to 1,137 pieces—probably the greatest cache of pre-Columbian ceramic art ever discovered. "Some appeared to have been deliberately arranged in symbolic tableaux, like figures of a Christmas crèche," Donnan and Alva wrote. "Musicians and prisoners, for example, ringed and faced nobler personages. Some trooped double file, while others appeared to be alone and apart, or placed adjacent to clusters of llama bones or sea shells."

Alva was puzzling over why such a huge collection of pots might have been put in the chamber when team members uncovered an even more provocative find—the skeleton of a man in a contorted, fetal-like position. Nearby lay a copper face mask and fragments of copper headdresses, but Alva, knowing that most Moche were buried with their legs extended and arms at their side, concluded they had probably belonged to someone else, as the deceased was probably a sacrificial victim, an accompaniment to a ritual offering.

Once it was established that nothing else remained in or beneath the pottery chamber, Alva and his team turned to another section of loose fill about 10 feet to the southeast of the first. Working from dawn until dusk over a period of weeks, the archaeologists removed the sand and stone, until, about 13 feet down, they found the skeleton of another male, this one about 20 years of age. From his habiliments of rotted cotton cloth and fragmentary copper armor, Alva theorized that he had perhaps been a warrior. Oddly, his feet were nowhere to be found, as if to symbolize his duty never to leave his post. Yet the archaeologists could not say for sure whether they had been amputated before or after his demise, and there was no sign of violent death. Alva referred to the warrior as the Guardian.

A few feet lower down the excavators once again came upon the gray, powdery residue of wood beams, suggesting that yet another chamber was below. From impressions left in the soil, Alva could tell that the beams, 17 in all, had measured as much as 13 feet in length and up to almost eight inches in diameter, and more important, that they had not been disturbed since they were originally set in place. Under them lay something that no archaeologist had ever seen before: eight clusters of bent copper straps, arranged in the shape of a rectangle more than seven feet long and four feet wide. Alva, familiar with the Moche practice of lashing together cane coffins using straw ropes, realized that the metal straps probably bound the wood planks of a coffin built for an exceptionally high-ranking member of the elite.

While the skull of a sacrifice grimaces in the foreground, the director of the Sipán excavations, Walter Alva, shows a small pot recovered from the site to an assistant. Buried with the victim was a dog, perhaps one of the spotted breed used in hunting and depicted on ceramics; its fragile bones can be seen at the skeleton's feet. The grave of the Warrior Priest lay to the left.

After recording and removing what was left of three planks that formed the box's cover, Alva and his team came across the remnants of three textile shrouds, two of which were adorned with sewn-on gilded copper platelets. Digging deeper, they exposed a number of lance points, feathered headdress ornaments, and the decomposed remains of a headdress topped with a gleaming gold ingot almost two inches in diameter and one-third of an inch thick.

The finding of the headdress preceded a deluge of additional discoveries, the first of which were a pair of cotton banners, the cloth still largely intact. Completely covered with almost 300 bits of gilded copper sheeting and adorned with small human figures also made from the sheet metal, they are thought to have once served some heraldic purpose, but their actual function remains a mystery, as nothing like them had been excavated before. Beneath the banners lay a piece of gilded copper sheeting in the shape of a headless human figure some two feet across, at the center of which stood the figure of a man wearing a nose ornament and a tiny necklace *(pages 108-109)*. Its function is unknown.

The archaeologists next turned up remains of a magnificent shirtlike cotton garment, every inch of which—like the banners—was completely covered with gilded copper platelets. Three colorful pectorals—broad, U-shaped decorations that upper-class Moche males wore around their necks—were found on top of it, and four more lay

Little more than a pink, white, and green smudge atop layers covering the decomposed skeleton of the Warrior Priest above, a pectoral posed a challenge to the archaeologists seeking to remove it whole. In order not to disrupt the pattern or mix the beads, whose connecting threads had turned to dust, the archaeologists gently cleaned them, then patted resin-soaked cotton on them and let it dry. The beads adhered, and the pectoral could be lifted away intact, ready for further cleaning and restringing in the laboratory. The finished piece is seen at above left, looking just as it did when it was interred 1,800 years ago with the Warrior Priest's body.

immediately underneath, along with three gold and one silver nose ornament and three pairs of circular earspools of exceptional beauty.

Adorning one of the pairs was a miniature warrior of hammered sheet gold. Wearing a turquoise tunic, the thumb-sized figure bore a nose ornament, a removable necklace of tiny gold beads crafted to depict owl heads, earspools of his own of turquoise and gold, a belt with crescent-shaped bells, and a headdress. In one hand he clenched a war club that could be loosened with a slight twist; on the other hung a removable circular shield. This "sprite," as Alva called him, was a brilliant example of the goldsmith's art and probably the finest piece of pre-Columbian jewelry yet to be discovered.

Ranked as one of the most exquisite pieces of jewelry ever to be found in the Americas, this gold and turquoise earspool only four inches high comes from the tomb of the Warrior Priest, whom it may even depict. The figure holds a detachable war club in the right hand. From the nose dangles a gold crescent-shaped ornament, while strung around the neck is a detachable necklace made up of tiny owl heads.

A U-shaped piece of sheet gold hammered into the shape of cheeks, chin, mouth, and upper neck covered the lower half of the skull of the tomb's occupant, which, after weeks of methodical excavation, finally came into view. Gently, the archaeologists lifted away the mask, revealing pieces of sheet gold fashioned to resemble two eyes, a nose, and a band of teeth; these had once covered the corresponding parts of the deceased. The face had apparently been painted red before burial, according to Moche custom, as traces of red pigment still clung to the skull.

Subjected to the crushing weight of the soil, the ancient bones had been reduced to little more than splinters. But John Verano, a physical anthropologist from the Smithsonian Institution in Washington, D.C., was able to determine that they belonged to a man in good health between the age of 35 and 45 who stood five feet five inches tall. His teeth, though he possessed a single cavity, showed little of the wear commonly seen in most Moche adults, a sign, perhaps, that he ate a special diet or that his food was prepared with exceptional care. There was no indication of the cause of death.

Around the shattered skeleton's neck, four necklaces glittered through the dancing motes of dust. The first was a simple ornament of spherical gold beads in graduated sizes, the second a circlet of 10 silver human-head beads, and the third a double strand of 10 peanut beads, half of them silver and half gold. The final necklace comprised 16 gold disks, each of which measured almost two inches in diameter. Remarkably, still-intact cotton straps held silver sandals in place

Layers of time-fused grave goods of the Old Lord of Sipán—who lived more than 200 years before the Warrior Priest—cover his remains in the photo at left. Dozens of red- and white-painted ceramic jars lie on either side, and on top rests a necklace comprising 10 beads, one of which gleams above after cleaning in the laboratory. Like the others, it is made of fine gold wire and sheet gold and depicts a spider with a scowling human face on its back.

on the man's feet. The shoes would have been so uncomfortable to walk in that the team concluded they must have been for ceremonial purposes only. In fact, scenes on Moche pottery commonly show lords being carried about on litters.

To Donnan, who visited Sipán at key stages of the excavation, the artifacts recovered so far offered unmistakable evidence that the occupant of the tomb had enjoyed high societal status and maybe even great political power. Alva, in fact, dubbed him the Lord of Sipán. But two additional discoveries soon made Donnan suspect that the lord had played some kind of religious or ceremonial role as well. The first was a pair of special knives—one gold, the other silver—found resting on the man's chest. Known as tumis, the knives appear in Moche art in depictions of ceremonial decapitations.

The second was a gold and silver scepter, or rattle *(page 40)*, over 13 inches long, found near the remains of the right hand. A masterpiece of metalworking, the staff was topped with a gold chamber resembling an inverted pyramid and bearing scenes of an elaborately dressed warrior raising a war club to the head of a naked prisoner. As soon as Donnan laid eyes on the artifact, he recalled later, the hair on the back of his neck stood straight out. "I remember just being almost speechless," he said, "because this is the rattle that is exclusively the property of this individual whom I had identified in Moche art 15 years before. And as I looked at it, gleaming in the late-afternoon sunlight—it's pure gold—I thought, 'My God, I know who this individual is! I know this guy. This is the guy I called Figure A.' "

The importance of the correlation, Donnan realized, was so great that he chose not to mention it to anyone until he could double-check his own writings on the sacrifice ceremony. Then he returned to the excavation site with a publication in hand and took Alva aside. "Walter," he said, "you're not going to believe this, but I think I know who this guy is."

Undoubtedly, he had been a Warrior Priest, the figure in Moche art who receives the goblet from Figure B, the Bird Priest. In the days ahead, Alva's team unearthed additional evidence to support this conclusion. The artifacts—a pair of gold crescent-shaped headdress decorations and two huge back flaps, one silver, the other gold—are featured in every depiction of Figure A. Both back flaps measured almost 18 inches in length, and the gold one—the largest Moche gold object ever recovered—weighed almost two pounds. The remains of feathers partially covered the larger of the headpiece adornments, a bladelike object of gleaming, polished gold almost two feet wide. Though badly decomposed, they were identified by North American ornithologist John O'Neil as belonging to the Chilean flamingo, a large, coral red bird native to the Andes.

Other signs of the Warrior Priest's eminence were to follow. Buried nearby were hundreds of ceramic pieces, two sacrificed llamas, a young child, three women between 15 and 20 years of age, and two men, aged 35 to 50, who had almost certainly been warriors themselves and possibly served as the priest's personal attendants. The disintegrated cane coffin of one of the men also held an especially tantalizing gift: the remains of a dog, suggestive of the animal shown at the feet of the Warrior Priest in depictions of the sacrifice ceremony.

By March 1988 the archaeologists had nearly completed excavating the tomb, and Alva and his team turned to two other promising excavation sites. The first was a simple pit located more than 16 feet beneath the pyramid's surface, in a section dated to the earliest phase of its construction (about the first century AD). There they found a tomb housing an ancient occupant wrapped in a straw mat and several textile shrouds, and grave goods similar to those found in the Warrior Priest's tomb: the remnants of banners, a number of ear and nose ornaments, four pectorals made of shell beads, two scepters about two feet long (one of gold, the other of silver), more than 20 back flaps of silver or gilded copper, and other items, including an exceptional collection of gold, silver, and gilded copper beads that once probably formed seven necklaces. Ten of the most striking beads measured about three and a quarter inches in diameter and featured a spider sitting on a web of exquisitely wrought gold wire spun across a shallow dish of sheet gold (page 106). Inside each were tiny gold balls that would have jingled as the wearer moved.

The artifacts had so much in common with those recovered previously that Alva felt certain some kind of link existed between the Warrior Priest and the newly found man, whom he called El Viejo Senor de Sipán—the Old Lord of Sipán. Alva and Donnan speculated that he may have been a Warrior Priest as well, only from a time 200 years before the crescent-shaped headdress and box-ended scepter of Figure A had become parts of his ritual paraphernalia.

The second excavation site was another area of fill located on a low, rectangular platform to the south of the pyramid's summit. There the archaeologists uncovered yet another tomb, this one belonging to a five-foot-two-inch Moche dignitary who died between

REMOVING THE CORROSION OF TIME

Many items in the Sipán tombs were heavily corroded when discovered, the result of oxidation of the copper in the gold-copper alloys from which they were produced.

Removing such corrosion is always a challenge. But thanks to a new method, some of the objects could be restored to glory (before and after, above

and below right) in fairly short order. Known as the plasma-chemical treatment, this procedure involves the creation of a plasma, a neutrally charged state of matter formed when an electrical charge passes through gases under low pressure.

In the case of the Sipán treasures, the gases employed in the German museum where the treatment was carried out between 1989 and 1992 were hydrogen and methane. The pieces were exposed to these gases for two hours at 392 degrees Fahrenheit, during which the oxidized layer of each was partially reduced and the remainder became so brittle it could be separated with relative ease.

Not all restorers approve of plasma treatment, since it destroys such ephemeral detail as pollen grains, feathers, and threads trapped in the oxidized metal. Evidence such as this can contribute to an understanding of the milieu in which the items were discovered and thus of the culture to which they belonged.

The Peruvian archaeologist Walter Alva, director of the Sipán excavations, still prefers careful mechanical techniques. He employs neutral solvents to soften the corrosion, then scrapes bits of it away with the aid of dental tools and an optic microscope. He sometimes leaves whole areas fairly untouched and applies consolidants—often acrylic resins— to these sections in order to secure any organic remains that might be imbedded there for future analysis.

the age of 35 and 45. Like both the Warrior Priest and the Old Lord, he was buried with a stunning array of gold, silver, and copper bells, nose and ear ornaments, necklaces *(pages 44-45),* and other items. But three in particular caught Donnan's eye.

The first was an 11-inch-long back flap similar in shape to those found in the Warrior Priest's tomb but consisting of two pieces that had been welded together—one of gold, the other of silver. The second was a copper cup, or goblet, found beside the man's right hand. The third was a magnificent gilded copper headdress almost two feet wide, at the center of which stood the head and body of an owl. The bird had inlaid white shell and turquoise eyes and bangle-covered arching bands for wings. Donnan had seen all three in Moche art many times before; they were characteristics of yet another major player in the sacrifice ceremony—Figure B, the Bird Priest.

Soon after this remarkable identification was made, a subsequent discovery forced Alva and Donnan to entertain an even more provocative notion, one that if true, would recast scholars' understanding of the very function of the pyramids at Sipán. About 30 feet west of the Bird Priest's tomb, the archaeologists uncovered the residue of wood beams that once covered several small, rectangular chambers. Upon excavation, the rooms were found to contain hundreds of ceramic vessels, a number of miniature copper war clubs and shields, and surprisingly, the relatively well preserved remains of llama and human bones, including entire hands and feet.

Since Moche art often shows the dismemberment of prisoners, Donnan suggested that the bones may have been trophies taken from actual sacrificial victims—and that the pyramid, shown to be the final resting place for two, or even three, participants in the sacrifice ceremony, may also have served as a site where the bloody rites themselves had been performed.

Alva and Donnan, compiling a catalog of the Sipán finds, noted that the Old Lord had been buried beneath a substantial pile of gilded sheet copper—parts of a headdress, beautifully crafted human and feline heads, the small figure of a warrior, and many others—all of which would have bedazzled graverobbers of an older time. "The hundreds of pieces of sheet copper mounded over the body," the archaeologists wrote, "would have appeared like solid gold at the time they were put in the tomb. They had corroded to a pale green color, almost completely obscuring the gold plating." Some had corroded so completely that no copper remained; the pieces shattered under the weight of the soil, burying their tiny amount of incorruptible gold under a heap of green residue.

Tombs looted by huaqueros in the early 1960s at Loma Negra, north of Lambayeque, yielded a similar collection of gilded copper heads, ear ornaments, small figures, and other items. They too surely looked like solid gold when buried but then slowly gave up their secret. North American archaeologist Heather Lechtman examined a number of the pieces under an electron microscope in 1982 and came away marveling at the sophistication and inventiveness of the Moche metalworkers. Using metallurgical techniques known today as depletion gilding and electrochemical replacement plating *(pages 44-45),* she discovered, the artisans had succeeded in creating gold coatings that were so even they looked like products of modern electrodeposits, and so thin that some could not be made out even when their cross sections were viewed at magnifications as great as 500. The effect may have deceived many a conquistador, who would have spirited off gleaming objects that when melted down proved to contain only traces of gold.

As to why the Moche worked their gold and copper as they did, an account written in 1596 by Sir Walter Raleigh describing metalworkers in Colombia may offer something of an answer. Most of their gold, he said, was secured not from gold-bearing rock but from lakes and rivers. "They gathered it in grains of perfect golde and in peeces as big as small stones, and they put to it a part of copper, otherwise they could not worke it, and they used a great earthern potte with holes round about it, and when they mingled the gold and copper together, they fastened canes to the holes, and so with the breath of men they

Knife in one hand and severed head in the other, the fearsome god known as the Decapitator is seen here in a gilded bell ornament from the tomb of the Warrior Priest. Recent scholarship has demonstrated that the figure is an anthropomorphized spider.

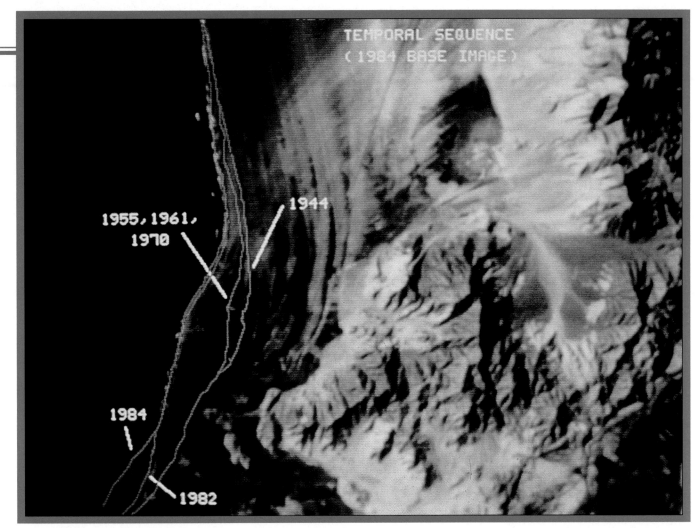

TEMPORAL SEQUENCE
(1984 BASE IMAGE)

1955, 1961, 1970

1944

1984

1982

Computerized, overlaid lines superimposed on high-altitude photographs of a section of Peruvian coastline near the Moche capital where the Pyramid of the Sun stands record the advances and retreats of a half-mile-long sand ridge that formed between 1955 and 1975. The ridge is the result of climatological changes, winds, an earthquake, storms, and flooding. Similar changes could have contributed to the demise of the Moche, causing sand dunes to move inland and bury the capital, forcing the inhabitants to move away.

increased the fire till the mettell ran, and then they cast it into moulds of clay and stones, and so make those plates and Images." A piece of Moche pottery confirms Raleigh's account *(page 36)*.

It was an energetic and ingenious operation performed by a vital and creative people. Yet by AD 800 the Moche had apparently disappeared, leaving their pyramids and sumptuous burials as markers of where they once lived. Scholars can only wonder why so brilliant a culture seems to have been extinguished so quickly. One explanation, advanced by North American anthropologist Michael E. Moseley, is that the Moche were overwhelmed by a series of natural cataclysms. He argues that a devastating earthquake may have set things off, disrupting water channels and rendering them useless and triggering landslides that dumped sand into the sea.

"The sand eventually washed ashore to create large dunes," Moseley suggests. "Propelled by the winds, the dunes moved inland. The result was a sand sea relentlessly inundating farms and villages." The dunes would have marched across the land, migrated into cities, buried huacas and canals, and silted up houses. After this, according to Moseley, came a period of drought, followed by two occurrences of the deadly weather system known as El Niño. The disturbance would have unleashed torrential rains and transformed the desert into a reeking swamp. Crops would have died, any remaining irrigation systems would have silted up, and mud-brick buildings would have dissolved. Indeed, archaeologists digging deep trenches in the vicinity of the Huaca del Sol and Huaca de la Luna in 1972 found the remains of ancient residences and other buildings buried under nearly 30 feet of flood-deposited sediment.

It is a dramatic story, yet it appears that more than just the climate may have contributed to the disappearance of the Moche. The historian Bartolomé de las Casas, writing in about 1550 of an era that had ended many centuries before, suggests that early Andean cultures, encompassing a geographical area many times greater in size than the Moche domain, may have weakened themselves in bloody altercations brought on by their continuous quest for water and productive soil. "This early period lasted about five or six hundred years," he wrote. "During this time the country was divided into a great number of chieftaincies, some larger than others but none of any great extent. . . . Between the peoples of adjacent communities there was a primitive kind of commerce whereby products of one kind were bartered for those of another. There was, therefore, some slight trade between neighboring states, but none at all between widely separated localities. These idyllic conditions lasted for some time, but later on wars and discords gradually came into being, chiefly provoked by questions relative to land and water-rights."

Gordon McEwan, the associate curator of the Denver Art Museum, thinks he knows who conquered or overthrew the Moche: the Wari, an imperial state that emerged in the highlands while the Moche went into decline on the north coast. And archaeologists, in fact, have discovered Wari ceremonial ceramics in the Huaca del Sol. But did the Wari invade the land of the Moche or did they move into a land already abandoned when a series of natural disasters entombed the Moche fields and buildings in sand?

Or could it be that, given the changes in circumstance inevitable to any civilization, the Moche survived the warfare and the shifting sands, absorbed outside influences, and matured into one generation after another? To compare a strong, proud face modeled in clay by a Moche artisan with a Peruvian Indian face of today is to see a keen likeness, and to wonder if the Moche ever died.

A HISTORY MODELED IN CLAY

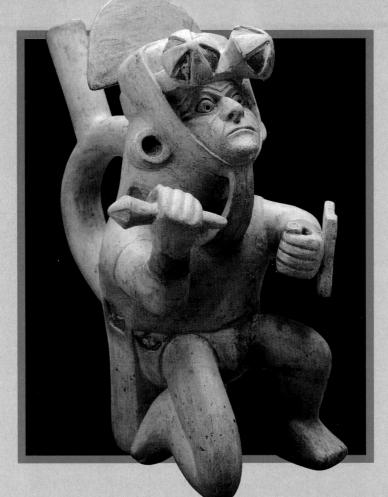

Few objects left behind by the Moche tell more about this vanished people than do the myriad decorated ceramic containers that have been unearthed over the years. The pottery was fashioned with an eye for artistry, detail, and even character—sculpted facial features, which appear on numerous pieces, were almost certainly those of real people. Moreover, Moche pottery was often embellished with finely delineated scenes of various activities, ceremonies, warfare, and animals that provide a tantalizingly intimate look at a culture that had no written language.

The vessels are commonly found in tombs of the elite. Scholars believe that they may also have been used by the living, often in rituals and commemorations rather than for everyday purposes: The characteristic hollow-handled stirrup spout, as seen on the back of the terra-cotta figure of the expressive kneeling warrior shown above, would have been unwieldy for routine household applications.

The artisans who crafted the pottery were highly skilled. And while they often employed turntables to slowly rotate their work, they lacked rapidly spinning potter's wheels. Their most basic technique was simple hand modeling, sometimes with the additional aid of a roundish stone or ceramic "anvil," which they held on the inside of a vessel while slapping the outside with a wooden paddle to give the clay shape. They also formed some of their wares by coiling long strands of clay up from a base.

A more elaborate means of production, frequently used to turn out large numbers of items, involved two-piece press molding. Using this method, the potter pushed wet clay into a pair of molds that formed the front and back of the pot or figurine. As the clay dried the molds were removed, the two halves were pressed and smoothed together, and a few finishing touches were applied. The result was a perfectly formed ceramic ready for painting and firing.

A SOCIETY OF RIGID CLASSES

The realistic human figures depicted so graphically on Moche pottery speak not only of the appearance and dress of the people, but also of the events and concerns that dominated their lives. Many pots, for example, are circled with depictions of elaborately garbed men bearing ornate staffs; sometimes the men are marching, or sometimes they are seated on thronelike platforms. Seen in the context of other portrayals of simply dressed people engaged in more mundane pursuits, these images reveal a highly stratified society with an elite class devoted to ritual and ceremony.

Interestingly, a large number of pots show individuals who are diseased or deformed. So realistic and graphic are some of these depictions that modern physicians often can look at them and diagnose the malady. And because many of these figures are well dressed, scholars have concluded that the sick and deformed probably had a special status in Moche culture.

Wielding ceremonial staffs, a procession of flamboyantly dressed members of the Moche elite adorns the sides of this stirrup-spouted terra-cotta pot; a view of the scene is shown below. Similar staffs have been found in Moche graves, and experts speculate that the objects were ritually tossed into the air and made to spin as the cord around the middle unwound.

This figure of a plainly dressed mother with a child strapped to her back (right) is typical of the depictions of women in Moche pottery. Some pots similar to this one feature a "child" who looks more like a small man, suggesting to some that even such seemingly simple domestic scenes may have had a deeper symbolic meaning.

The man shown in this stirrup-spout pot (left) is missing part of his nose and upper lip, the result of either leprosy or leishmaniasis, both of which cause an eating away of tissues. In the victim's permanent disfigurement the Moche may have seen the rot of death.

115

THE STRANGE WORLD OF ANIMALS

Animals played a large part in Moche culture and were frequently portrayed in pottery. Among the many creatures that appear on the ceramics are guinea pigs, deer, llamas, sea lions, and a variety of fish, all native to the region inhabited by the Moche. Other, more exotic animals—among them toucans and monkeys—are seen as well, suggesting to archaeologists that there was a certain amount of trade with adjacent jungly areas such as modern-day Ecuador. It is likely that these imported animals were kept as pets.

Although the creatures are often presented realistically, sometimes roaming in their natural habitats, they are occasionally shown symbolically. Human figures, for example, appear with the heads of owls or foxes, possibly representing shamans or priests who have donned animal masks as part of their magical practices. And elaborately clothed hunters pursue animals such as deer or sea lions in such a way as to suggest that the pursuit has a ritual meaning that transcends the mere quest for meat.

Letting out a shriek, this stirrup-spouted monkey is wearing earrings, similar to those worn by the Moche themselves, and clutching a melonlike pepino fruit. Monkeys were trained to assist in the harvesting of fruit from trees.

Finely modeled antlers and ears surmount this realistically sculpted deer-head bowl. Deer apparently were not commonly used as food, as their bones do not show up in any quantity in refuse deposits. More likely, the animals were hunted for ceremonial reasons, as suggested by images on pots of elaborately clad Moche in hot pursuit of their elusive white-tailed quarry.

Club in hand, a sea-lion hunter nears his quarry on the elaborate vessel at right. The round object in the animal's mouth represents the beach pebbles swallowed by sea lions for digestive purposes and recovered when the creatures were killed. Believed to have curative powers, such stones are also seen below in the hunting scene drawn on the sides of the pot.

SHADOWY REALMS OF RITUAL

Deities and the variety of rituals associated with them were among the Moche potters' favorite themes. One of the most common deities has a human body and jaguarlike fangs, and is frequently shown in scenes of sacrifices or in the context of ocean waves or mountain peaks, both of which seem to have loomed large in the Moche view of the supernatural.

Healing ceremonies were of paramount importance in Moche culture, and such rites are often depicted in pottery. The scenes usually show the curer, accompanied by various charms and plant products and sometimes with the head of an animal thought to have magical powers, hovering over the prostrate patient.

Possibly the most puzzling of all the activities commonly pictured on the pottery involves lines of energetic runners wearing ornate headgear and carrying what appear to be small bags. Scholars have tried in vain to determine for certain what the runners were doing. So far, they can only agree that whatever it was, it was very important to the Moche.

His waist cinched with a serpent belt, a fanged god looks on as the body of a hapless mortal is borne on the crest of an ocean wave topping a step motif that may represent mountain peaks. Two additional human figures are shown on the steps. All three are probably sacrificial offerings.

A healer—either an owl-faced god or a masked human—grips a slice of hallucinogenic cactus and prepares to minister to the patient shown lying to the right. The four rows of beadlike objects painted in front of the healer are strings of dried espingo seeds, still used in north coastal Peru to treat psychic problems and stomachaches.

Grimly intent on their mysterious goal, Moche runners dash eternally around this graceful stirrup-spout bottle. Some scholars suggest that the runners are whisking bags of seeds to plant symbolically in conquered territories; others propose that the bags contain lima beans that were somehow used for communications, recordkeeping, or foretelling the future.

PORTRAYALS OF WAR AND JUSTICE

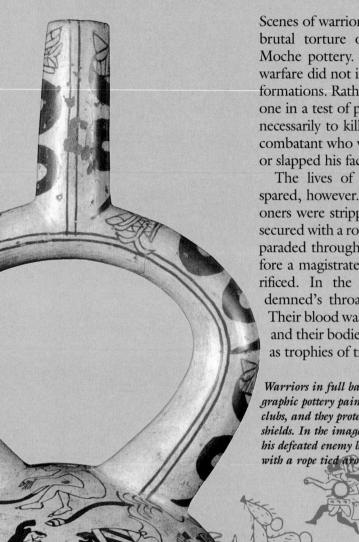

Scenes of warriors and combat—and of the sacrifice or brutal torture of prisoners—are quite common in Moche pottery. From these images, scholars assume warfare did not involve the engagement of large troop formations. Rather, individual warriors grappled one to one in a test of personal valor. And the object was not necessarily to kill the enemy: Victory could go to the combatant who whacked his adversary with a war club or slapped his face or grabbed him by the hair.

The lives of warriors thus vanquished were not spared, however. In the hands of the enemy, the prisoners were stripped of their weapons and clothes and secured with a rope around their necks. They were then paraded through throngs of the victors and taken before a magistrate, who ordered the captives to be sacrificed. In the ceremony that followed, the condemned's throats were cut with ceremonial knives. Their blood was then drunk by priests and attendants, and their bodies were cut to pieces and put on display as trophies of triumph.

Warriors in full battle dress struggle hand to hand in this graphic pottery painting. Their main weapons are war clubs, and they protect themselves with small round or square shields. In the image directly below, a victorious combatant grips his defeated enemy by the hair; at far right, a naked prisoner with a rope tied around his neck awaits his inevitable fate.

A Moche warrior grips an enemy by the hair while hitting him in the head with a formidable club. The crescent-shaped object swinging from the victim's waist resembles a sacrificial knife but is really a back flap designed to protect his lower back.

In this vivid tableau, a vulture cleans out the eye socket of a writhing prisoner, skin flayed from his face, who has been bound securely to a tree trunk. Scholars believe that the victim was probably not a captive warrior—whose sacrifice would have been carried out with some dignity—but a criminal, possibly a thief.

THE PARACAS AND NAZCA CULTURES: GLOWING ACHIEVEMENTS IN A DESERT

Offerings to ancient gods may once have been carried along the 98-foot-long Nazca geoglyph, dubbed the owl man, at left. The ritual trek was repeated in making this time exposure, the walker bearing nothing more sacred than a flashlight.

The beauty of the textiles was unmistakable, their artistry as obvious to the untrained eye as it was to any expert's. But even as more and more of the exquisite fabrics found their way into collections in and outside of Peru early in the 20th century, their source remained a mystery. Only the *huaqueros* who were now plundering a new trove of ancient grave sites could have accounted with any honesty for the origin of their purloined goods. But the graverobbers were not being paid to be honest, and their eager customers would hardly be so foolish as to show curiosity about the provenience of the items they had purchased.

Some scholars were curious, however, among them the Peruvian archaeologist Julio C. Tello, who in the 1930s would argue that the imposing ceremonial complex known as Chavin de Huantar stood at the center of the far-flung, ancient Chavin culture. But in 1914, his career just starting, he got his first look at the splendidly embroidered tunics and mantles that would come to be known as the Paracas textiles. Suspecting they were the artifacts of a previously unknown South American culture, Tello followed their trail from the antiquities shops of Lima into the Peruvian highlands and eventually, spurred by false rumors spread by the huaqueros, to centuries-old cemeteries in the Nazca, Ica, and Pisco Valleys, about 180 miles south of Lima. To his frustration, the only ancient textiles he came across were those that had already fallen into the hands of collectors.

By the summer of 1925 his colleague, North American archaeologist Alfred L. Kroeber, had narrowed the search to the arid Paracas Peninsula, a small, wind-swept appendage of Peru that juts westward into the Pacific Ocean between the Pisco and Ica Valleys. A few weeks later Tello persuaded Juan Quintana, a guard at a local fertilizer company and a well-known huaquero, to divulge the precise source of the textiles. On the overcast afternoon of July 26, 1925, Tello's decade-long quest came to an end, as the professional archaeologist followed the professional graverobber first to a site called Arena Blanca and then to Cerro Colorado, the terraced, mauve-colored, granite outcrop that looms as the physical and spiritual focus of the peninsula. All around lay the calling cards of Quintana and his fellow looters, including overlooked fragments of textiles, discarded pieces of pottery, and disinterred human bones and skulls.

Tello loaded his car with artifacts from both locations and returned to Lima, confident that like the huaqueros who had preceded him, he had found his own El Dorado. He immediately made plans to excavate the Paracas sites systematically, and within a month, he and his assistant, the Peruvian archaeologist Toríbio Mejía Xesspe, began work. At two spots on the north side of Cerro Colorado, they turned up persuasive signs of long-ago habitation—the foundations of 20 domestic structures, baskets, gourd containers, panpipes and needles fashioned from wood and bone, and other artifacts, as well as the remains of such foods as yuca (cassava), corn, peanuts, and fish.

More important, the archaeologists directed their energies to three cemeteries. The first of these was situated along the northern edge of Cerro Colorado, at Arena Blanca. It contained 13 burial areas, the largest of which huaqueros called Cabeza Larga, or Long Head, after the elongated skulls they had turned up in their diggings. Tello and Mejía uncovered the remains of more than 130 men, women, and children. Each corpse was seated, its knees flexed and tucked under its chin, and each had been wrapped in textiles to create a large, cone-shaped funerary bundle. Many of the bundles were surrounded by simple but well-made monochromatic pottery and other grave goods, apparently to ensure that the deceased would enjoy the comforts of home in the next world—or that upon arrival, he or she would have gifts to present to the gods.

The second cemetery lay less than a mile to the south of Arena Blanca on the rocky summit of Cerro Colorado itself. Tello dubbed the site Cavernas because he and Mejía discovered a collection of bottle-shaped, cavernlike tombs that had been cut into three terraces on the hilltop. Some were found to contain more than 30 corpses, all of which rested within individual funerary bundles consisting of many layers of wrapped cloth; one tomb even held the body of a dog, wound, like its human counterparts, in fabric. There was pottery, too, and other grave goods, but the ceramics—pieces that were not one color only, but polychromatic—differed markedly in style from those discovered at the previous sites.

Variations could also be seen in the funerary bundles, as evidenced by the number of textiles used to wrap the corpses; the differences were apparent not only between the Cavernas bundles and those of Arena Blanca, but also among the Cavernas bundles themselves. At Arena Blanca, for example, most bodies were wrapped in a single plain cloth, an indication that the various cemeteries of Arena Blanca may have been reserved for the poorer members of Paracas society. Similarly, some of the Cavernas corpses were wrapped in only a rough cotton sheet, but others were enshrouded in one or two plain mantles and arrayed with simple ornaments. A few were bound up in even more textiles distinguished by their greater decorativeness. Sometimes gold ornaments lay tucked in the bundles or in the mouth of the deceased.

The disparity between rich and poor was even more obvious at the third of the Paracas cemeteries, located along the northern slopes of Cerro Colorado, between the summit and Arena Blanca. Excavations started in October 1927 unearthed hundreds of simple burials there and as many as 30 opulent ones, suggesting that the site may have been the necropolis, or special burial place, of a Paracas elite, though some scholars question this notion. Tello and Mejía even named the site the Necrópolis of Wari Kayan, or "ancestral temple."

The archaeologists were pleased to discover that the huaqueros had not disturbed the dead in this cemetery. The bodies had been placed in clusters in and around the foundations of houses, rather than in bottle-shaped tombs as at Cavernas, and they were far more numerous than at the Cavernas site. The excavators came across so many burials, in fact, that once the bulky bundles had been freed of their mantles of dirt and debris, Mejía took one look at the bundle-studded slope and likened it to a field of potatoes at harvesttime.

Because the style of pottery discovered in the Necrópolis burials was the same as that found at Arena Blanca, and different from that of the Cavernas ceramics, Tello became convinced that two distinct social or ethnic groups once lived on the Paracas Peninsula. Differences in the textiles found in the cemeteries—and in the methods used to flatten the heads of the occupants, a practice known as cranial deformation—seemed to support his conclusion. He named the cultures Cavernas and Necrópolis. Years later, after his pioneering work at Chavin de Huantar, he would argue that the pair formed a single *"cultura Paracas"* that had flourished on the peninsula from 600 to 175 BC and was in turn part of what he called the *"cultura matriz,"* the mother culture of the central Andean region.

Raw materials used to make the Paracas grave goods—obsidian and llama, alpaca, and vicuna wool from the highlands, feathers from the rain forest, spondylus shells from the north—also revealed that the peninsula had been part of an extensive trade network; the area may even have served as the hub of a local trade in salt or in salted fish. Whatever the source of its wealth, the Paracas culture would eventually give rise to an even more sophisticated branch of Tello's mother culture, Nazca. Evolving along the southern coast of Peru around 100 BC, Nazca endured until about AD 600. Its cultural legacy includes superb pottery and textiles, but its most memorable achievement consists of the so-called Nazca lines, the immense ground drawings, or geoglyphs, that have puzzled generations of scholars and long tickled the popular imagination.

Few places on earth seem as inhospitable to human habitation as the coast of Peru. For much of its length it is a desert, the dryness relieved here and there by seasonally fed rivers that descend from the

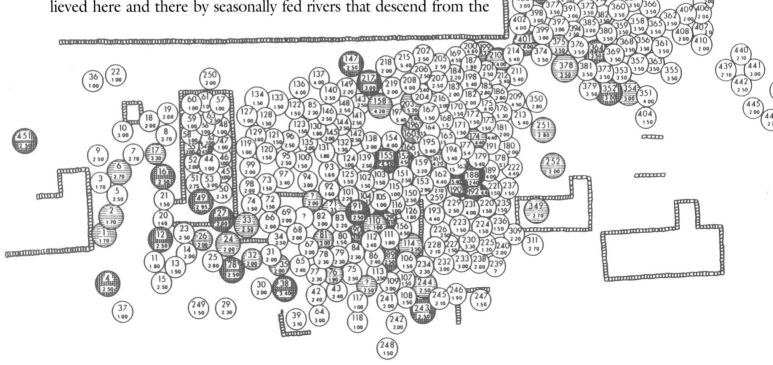

LARGE BUNDLE

MEDIUM BUNDLE

SMALL BUNDLE

snowcapped Andes and transform the desert valleys into oases. But drier still is the Paracas Peninsula, where no rivers run at all, rain almost never falls, and the landscape is nearly devoid of vegetation. Here, the only reliable source of water lies in the ground itself, in ancient aquifers. Although nights are invariably cool and foggy throughout the year, broiling daytime temperatures are the rule in summer, as are the daily late-afternoon sandstorms that scour the area until dusk, then subside as suddenly as they arose. These sandstorms, known locally as *paracas*, from the Quechua word for "sand falling like rain," gave the peninsula its name.

The lack of precipitation has had the eerie effect of rendering the desert floor virtually changeless, so much so that in many places any marks made on it survive for centuries. No doubt the most striking examples of this phenomenon are the Nazca ground drawings, but newer prints—tracks made by waffle-soled boots and by the tires of all-terrain vehicles—will likely remain visible for just as long. The aridity has proved to be beneficial for the desert's rich pre-Columbian archaeological record, preserving 2,000-year-old corpses and providing a benign environment for artifacts that would otherwise be perishable, such as textiles.

Julio Tello would discover as much in the course of his excavations atop and around Cerro Colorado. By the time he completed his initial Necrópolis excavations in April 1928, a total of 429 bundles had been uncovered. Trucked to Lima in the back of a Dodge pickup, they were temporarily housed in the Museum of Peruvian Archaeology before being moved again to their current home in the National Museum of Anthropology and Archaeology. There Tello oversaw the unwrapping of more than 40 of the largest bundles *(pages 128-129)*, all of which contained the corpses of men of advanced age. Each bundle was numbered and tagged, as was each textile and each object contained in the bundle.

Since that time, the artifacts have had an uneasy rest. Removed from the dry desert environment that had preserved them through the ages, and subjected to the dampness, mold, and insects that characterize all urban settings, many suffered more damage in the decades since their excavation than they had in the 2,000 years before their discovery. Worse still, a number of the identifying tickets were accidentally lost or switched over the years, making it impossible to associate some grave goods with the bundles that had originally held them. And regrettably, it was not until 1959, more than

This crowded diagram delineates burials in section A, one of two parts of the Necrópolis of Wari Kayan on the slopes of Peru's Cerro Colorado. Circles denote the more than 300 mummy bundles recovered from the section in the late 1920s by Peruvian archaeologists Julio C. Tello and Toríbio Mejía Xesspe. The upper number in each circle represents the size, in meters, of the individual bundles, classified as small, medium, or large. The lower number indicates the depth, again in meters, at which the top of each bundle first appeared. (Some bundles were uncovered more than 15 feet down.) The angular shapes mark the remains of subterranean chamber walls.

30 years after the fact and 12 years after Tello's death, that the first report on the Paracas excavations was published, and it described only a fraction of the total discovery. Before then, several newspaper articles and a notice given at a 1928 international congress of Americanists were the only published accounts of Tello and Mejía's work.

Although there was no comprehensive accounting of the archaeological context in which the discoveries were made, and no written records were left behind by the Indians themselves, the funerary bundles nevertheless reveal much about Paracas society. To be sure, Tello and Mejía recognized that the textiles and their embroideries had a story to tell as soon as they unwrapped the first funerary bundles. Their early interpretations have since been augmented by the studies of other archaeologists and art historians, who have focused their efforts on specific aspects of the Paracas finds, examining recovered pottery and comparing designs, for example, or theorizing about the inherent symbolism of the Paracas textiles. From this research, a picture of life long ago on the Paracas Peninsula is just now beginning to emerge.

Most experts agree that the cultures identified by the three cemeteries enjoyed their heyday from roughly 600 to 175 BC and that the Cavernas graveyard—the only one of the trio that was not situated on or among earlier graves or structures—is the oldest. It dates to the

These pencil, ink, and watercolor drawings by the Peruvian artist Hernan Ponce Sanchez portray some of the stages in the unwrapping of mummy bundle 451 from the Wari Kayan Necrópolis. As the plain cloth and colorful embroidered garments were peeled off, there was one final wrapping, a simple brown cotton fabric. Inside was the naked body of a gray-haired man over 60 years old. With his legs flexed in a seated position, he was tucked snugly into a funerary basket. Swathing the dead in layers of textiles created a microenvironment in the hot sand, which helped to dry and thus preserve their bodies.

end of the Early Horizon, the period marked by the dramatic spread of the Chavín culture from about 900 to 200 BC. For their part, the later cemeteries at Arena Blanca and Necrópolis were probably contemporary with each other. They date from 450 to 175 BC, a time that spans the Early Horizon and its successor phase, the Early Intermediate Period. All three cemeteries may even have been in use simultaneously for a spell at the end of the Early Horizon.

Such conclusions are based partly on the results of radiocarbon dating and partly on artifact associations, specifically by comparison of pottery recovered from the Paracas sites with finds collected in the nearby Ica Valley, for which a chronology had painstakingly been worked out. It also seems likely, based on the available evidence, that the Cavernas culture got its start as a loose network of fishing villages whose residents buried their dead in cavernlike tombs atop Cerro Colorado. Toward the end of the Early Horizon, the area around Arena Blanca gradually became the focus of the various settlements, and more and more buildings encroached on the northern slopes of Cerro Colorado. This led to a change in burial customs and a shift in burial sites: No longer would bodies be laid to rest at Cavernas, and only rarely would they be interred in cavernlike tombs. Instead, the people of Arena Blanca would now bury their dead around abandoned structures in Cabeza Larga and the smaller burial areas of Arena Blanca.

Changes such as these, together with the development of new pottery and textile styles, apparently signaled the influence of an emerging culture, Tello's Necrópolis. But whether this was a distinct

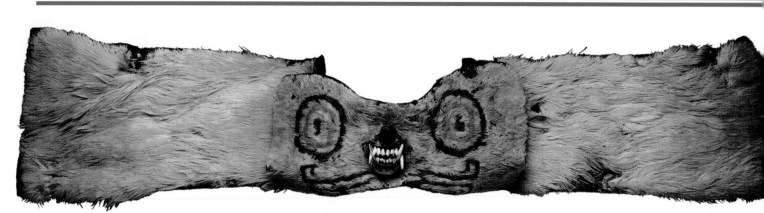

society that coexisted for a time with the old Cavernas culture, probably at the end of the Early Horizon Period, or was merely the next step in the natural evolution of Cavernas, the archaeologists cannot yet definitively ascertain.

Scholars associate a distinct pottery style with each of the two cultures identified by Tello and Mejía. Cavernas-style ceramics, now generally referred to simply as Paracas pottery, have been found not only at the Cavernas cemetery on the peninsula, but also in the nearby Ica, Chincha, and Pisco Valleys. In fact, a number of scholars consider the Ica Valley to be the heartland of Paracas pottery and further theorize that the valley's influence spread to the peninsula later.

    In general, Paracas pottery took the form of graters, bowls, and distinctive bottles with double spouts and bridging handles. These were often painted with rich resin pigments after firing, and as many as four or five different colors were employed on a single vessel. Lines were incised to separate the areas of color or to accent the various motifs—including banded geometric designs, feline figures, and slit-eyed human beings—that are characteristic of the style. Other Paracas ware featured dots, striping, or crosshatched lines created by a technique known as negative painting. After firing, the designs were marked on the pots with slip, a thick suspension of clay and water. Next, the vessels were darkened all over, either by exposing them to dense smoke or by covering them with an organic black pigment, most likely plant extracts, and scorching them. Subsequent soaking removed only the slip, which protected the light original surface color from the effects of the pigment or smoke.

    The pottery style associated with the Necrópolis culture, known as Topará, is thought to have its roots in the Cañete Valley to the north, though pieces have been found in the Chincha and Pisco Valleys as well. It is distinguished by a comparatively reserved mono-

The Paracas-style adornment above is part of a headdress. The face is fashioned from the skin of a fox head with the teeth and nose intact. Plumes from the blue-and-yellow macaw and other tropical birds were glued with resin onto the skin and the cotton cloth side pieces. Green and orange feathers represent eyes and whiskers. Such feathers would have been obtained through trade with peoples living in forested areas east of the Andes.

chrome appearance. Usually cream- or orange-colored and otherwise undecorated, Topará-style pottery is nevertheless far more elegant than its Paracas-style counterpart, and its extraordinarily thin walls and precise modeling represent a significant advance in the level of craftsmanship. Because of this, some scholars suggest that the style signals a distinct culture that experienced what North American archaeologist Helaine Silverman has referred to as "intense and fluid contact" with Paracas culture.

Paradoxically, the trend toward simplicity of form and the restraint in the use of color that are so evident in the Topará pottery of the Necrópolis culture did not extend to the Necrópolis textiles, which are brightly colored, intricately embroidered, and truly magnificent masterpieces. Such weaving was clearly the focus of the creative talents of the early peoples buried on the Paracas Peninsula. "The quality and quantity of textiles surpass the technical skill and numbers of all other artifacts recovered from the excavated burials,"

Snakelike creatures slither across the face of this Paracas ceramic mask found at Chongos in Peru's Pisco River valley. It probably represents the Oculate Being, so called by archaeologists because of the large, hollow eyes. Although only a few such clay masks have turned up, similar images occur on painted mummy-bundle masks placed over the wrapped faces of the dead, and on Ica Valley pottery.

writes North American art historian Anne Paul, "and leave little doubt as to the paramount importance of weaving in this culture."

Moreover, though these textiles are known today chiefly as wrappings for the dead, the funerary bundles also contain a variety of garments. Among these are ponchos and headbands, turbans and tunics, mantles, skirts, and loincloths, all of which were elaborately embroidered with wool yarn. Most spectacular were cotton mantles that often measured as much as four by nine feet. Plainer mantles, such as those used in some poorer bundles, could be even larger, sometimes measuring up to 11 feet in width.

Exactly how such textiles were created remains something of a mystery, since neither parts nor images of looms have been uncovered at any of the Paracas sites. It is possible, however, that portable backstrap looms *(page 94)* were used to create the smaller garments. Larger textiles could not have been woven on these looms, since the arm span of the weaver limited the maximum width of the cloth.

Cavernas textiles were simpler in design and more subtle in color. Typical motifs—ranging from interlocking snakelike and fishlike figures to felines and human effigies—were usually woven or looped into the fabric rather than embroidered. Not only were Necrópolis textiles more colorful than the Cavernas cloths, they were also exquisitely embroidered. Design motifs were similarly ambitious, depicting a menagerie of animals, as well as plants, human figures, and mythical creatures and deities. Some forms appear often enough that they have been assigned names by researchers. One of these, known as the Ecstatic Shaman *(pages 154-155)*, appears on dozens of Necrópolis-era garments. True to its name, it takes the form of a priestlike figure, its body arched, its head thrown back and arms extended, as though caught in a moment of wild abandon.

Status was seemingly as important in death as it was in life, as evidenced by the comparative wealth of the largest Necrópolis bundles, thought to have contained members of the elite. Each cadaver was provided with a full wardrobe of clothing interleaved in yards and yards of wrapping cloths, which were bunched at the top and wound with a rope to create a topknot. The corpse was then shrouded in one or more mantles and perhaps enveloped in still another wrapping cloth. The end result may have approached five feet in diameter and stood an equal number of feet high, creating, in the words of Paul, nothing less than a "stratified hill of cloth."

The elaborately embroidered designs on the apparel may have

conveyed information about the wearer's status, ritual duties, or occupation, as well as the details of that individual's lineage. Likewise, images symbolizing long-cherished cultural values and beliefs may also have been incorporated into the cloth *(pages 151-157)*. Some motifs were apparently so important they were retained from textile to textile for as long as seven generations without major iconographic or formal changes. To Paul, the embroidered garments are "the 'texts' of Paracas culture." The problem, of course, lies in translating those texts into words, especially when even the twist of the yarn in a particular piece of fabric may be imbued with hidden meaning.

Recent research, however, is making headway in deciphering the iconography of the Paracas textiles. Closer studies of weaving styles, embroidery stitches, and dyeing techniques, for example, have resulted in a textile sequence that has proved even more useful than the Ica Valley pottery sequence in establishing a chronology for the Paracas sites and in dating recovered artifacts. Furthermore, a careful examination of the textiles in individual bundles has allowed scholars to discern broad themes encoded in the Paracas garments, identifying felines, for example, as possible metaphors for the terrestrial world and fish for the sea, or finding evidence for decapitation in the ubiquitous depiction of trophy heads.

If mystery still shrouds much of Paracas culture, obscurity also cloaks the Nazca culture, its direct descendant, and partly for similar reasons. Like those buried on the Paracas Peninsula, the Indians who gave rise to the Nazca culture were a farming and fishing people who created fine, richly symbolic polychrome pottery and wove beautiful textiles that one historian has theorized might also encode "important and sacred knowledge." In addition, the Nazca people—and, apparently, the groups that preceded and followed them—left behind even more tantalizing artwork, their enormous ground drawings, or geoglyphs, scratched onto the surface of the coastal desert overlooking the Nazca Valley. Some of the geometric ones are miles long and arrow-straight, deviating, according to an estimate by North American astronomer Gerald Hawkins, no more than four yards per mile *(pages 140-141)*. Others zigzag across the desert floor, while still others are laid out in tightly coiled spirals or in the shapes of living things.

Located less than 100 miles southeast of the Paracas Peninsula and 38 miles inland from the Pacific coast, the Nazca Valley is just

SIGNS OF THE TIMES: EMBLEMS AND SYMBOLS EMBROIDERED ON GARMENTS

In their attempts to find meanings in the embroidered designs on the textiles from Paracas mummy bundles, Andean scholars have subjected the designs to detailed analysis—and in the process have come to appreciate the enormous skill and artistry that were required to create them.

Examples from the Necrópolis of Wari Kayan display the three embroidery styles pictured below—linear, broad line, and block color. In the block-color style, the embroiderer outlined the images in thread, then filled them in with different hues. The countless stitches allowed humans, supernatural beings, animals, and plants to be rendered in considerable detail. Indeed, the humans and supernatural beings wear tunics and ornaments and carry fans, staffs, and slings similar to some that have been found in the bundles.

When employing the linear style, the embroiderer reversed the process: As she stitched in the background, the images developed as negative forms and were filled in using multicolored parallel rows of horizontal, vertical, or diagonal stitches. The broad-line style was achieved by running multiple rows of the same color stitches so closely together that broad lines or bands emerged.

Linear and broad-line designs are typically more abstract than the block-color images; instead of specific characteristics of a particular species, for example, they show generic types. In both the linear and broad-line styles the images often consist of stick figures with the costumes and adornments generalized, making interpretation difficult.

Still, it seems likely to at least one scholar, North American art historian Anne Paul, that the artfully contrived linear and broad-line images may well have conveyed various meanings. Among the possibilities would be the wearer's rank, role, and occupation, as well as information about his mythical ancestors, his clan's name, and other important details of his lineage.

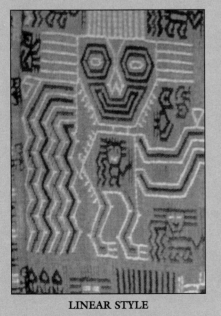

LINEAR STYLE

BROAD-LINE STYLE

BLOCK-COLOR STYLE

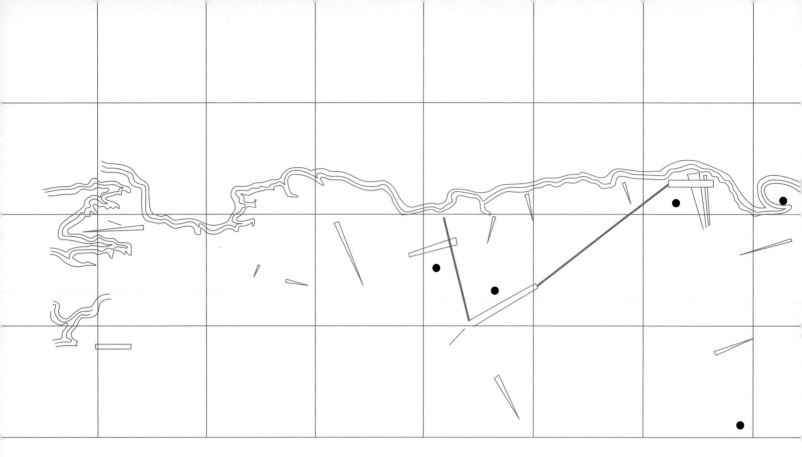

one of a number of watered coastal valleys in which life flourishes in an otherwise harsh and barren desert. Between these valleys lie wide, level plateaus, one of which rises from the Nazca Valley to form a broad plain, the Pampa Colorada, some 30 miles long and 15 miles wide. No ordinary plain, the Pampa Colorada is a natural blackboard, a flat surface of stones and gravel whose exposed faces have been turned reddish brown by oxidation, a result of the area's morning dew, daytime heat, and nighttime cold. It is on this blackboard that ancient peoples "drew" the famous Nazca geoglyphs. Primarily by assessing the age of pottery found on or near the geoglyphs, scholars now know that most of the lines date to the Early Intermediate Period, about 200 BC to AD 600. The inhabitants of the area selectively removed portions of the desert pavement to expose the lighter underlying soil, then used the dark rocks to line the light areas, heightening the contrast between the two.

As chance would have it, two of the archaeologists associated with the discovery of the Paracas sites also played a role in bringing these desert drawings to light. The men, Alfred Kroeber and Toríbio Mejía Xesspe, were part of an expedition that was excavating a site near Nazca in September 1926. Noticing a hill nearby and hoping that the low angle of the late-afternoon sun would bring any otherwise imperceptible archaeological remains into sharp relief, the two scholars scrambled up the rocky slope and surveyed the surrounding desert. What they saw was even more surprising than the ruins they

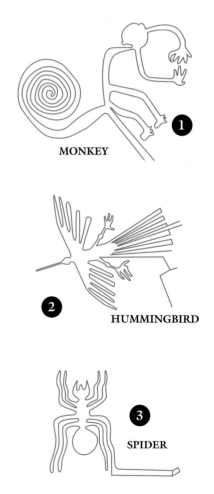

MONKEY **1**

HUMMINGBIRD **2**

SPIDER **3**

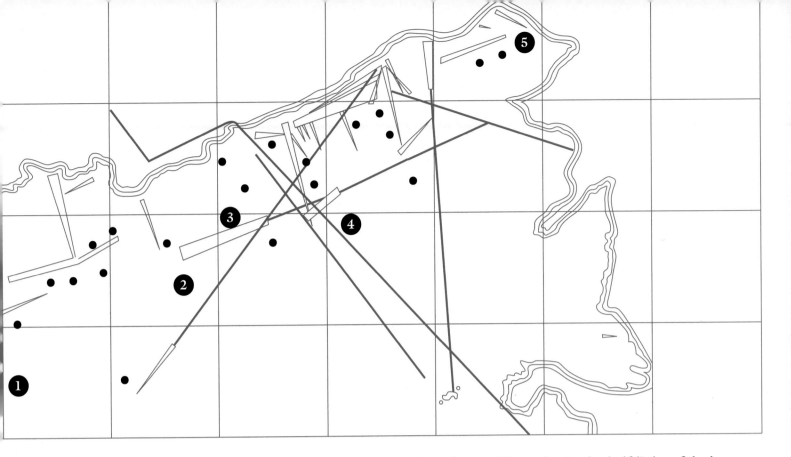

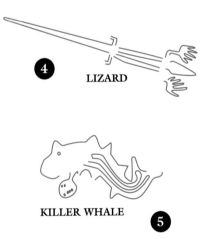

4 LIZARD

KILLER WHALE **5**

This schematic map shows the 15-square-mile area of Peru's Pampa de San José in which most of the surviving ground drawings of flora and fauna by the Nazca are found, along with many of the lines and geometric shapes they left. The dots mark sites of the figures, as do the five circled numbers, which are keyed to the examples above and at left. Among these five, the killer whale is the smallest, with a length of 80 feet, and the lizard is the longest, at 495 feet.

had hoped to see. Below them, plain as day in the half-light of dusk, a welter of lines seemed to chalk the blackboard of the desert.

Curiously, neither Kroeber nor Mejía thought much of the markings, which they wrote off as the remains of ancient irrigation channels. Even so, both men did make notes of their initial impressions of what would later be popularly known as the Nazca lines, and Mejía's became the basis of a report he would publish more than a decade later.

By then Mejía had decided that the lines had nothing to do with irrigation after all but were vaguely ceremonial in nature. By that time, too, the Nazca lines were attracting widespread attention, thanks largely to the introduction of scheduled airline flights over the Nazca desert and the use of aerial photography. Only then could the lines be seen in their entirety, and only then were individual drawings finally recognized for what they are: not only geometric shapes, but also human, animal, and plant forms.

Inspired by Mejía's report and by a growing number of newspaper accounts, the North American geographer and historian Paul Kosok determined to see the ground drawings for himself. Accompanied by his wife, he traveled to Peru in June 1941 and ventured out onto the pampa a few miles south of the city of Palpa. Almost immediately the Kosoks spotted one line, then another, and eventually whole complexes of lines, some of them centered on hilltops and punctuated by curious piles of stones. But the most startling of their

discoveries came that evening, when they happened to observe that the sun was setting along the very axis of one of the lines. Suddenly it occurred to Kosok that the date was June 21, the winter solstice in the Southern Hemisphere. "With a great thrill," he later wrote, "we realized at once that we had apparently found the key to the riddle."

The key that Kosok imagined he had found was an alleged link between the lines and calendrical and astronomical observations that had supposedly been made by the Indians. Kosok suggested that when viewed as a whole the lines formed an enormous calendar, with individual lines pointing to important astronomical positions at the horizon, such as the rising and setting points of the sun on the solstices and equinoxes.

Convinced that he had discovered what he called the "largest astronomy book in the world," Kosok was not at all shy about sharing his enthusiasm with anyone willing to listen. In his audience was Maria Reiche, a German-born student of mathematics and astronomy who was then living in Lima and working for Kosok as a translator. She not only accepted Kosok's astronomical calendar, but would later argue that it might have been critical to the survival of an agricultural people that lived on the edge of one of the world's driest deserts, allowing them to anticipate the arrival of the seasons or the return of the water to the rivers, or even to predict eclipses. Reiche immediately recognized her life's calling in the mysterious Nazca ground drawings. "The gods had ordained my journey and the course of my work," she would later recall.

With Kosok due to go back to the United States, Reiche agreed to pick up where he had left off and to return to the desert in time for the summer solstice on December 21. By year's end in 1941 she claimed to have identified no fewer than 16 solstice lines. She further maintained that many of the lines were parallel, an indication,

Guardian of the geoglyphs, Maria Reiche at 73 sweeps an enigmatic form in the desert. For more than four decades she mapped thousands of the Nazca ground drawings, surveying and charting them and maintaining the figures by brushing and otherwise clearing away debris.

she believed, that the "primitive intellectuals" who produced the lines must have deliberately sighted extremely distant objects—including possibly the midsummer sun—from a number of widely dispersed vantage points.

Encouraged by Kosok, Reiche next set out to plot the rising and setting points of the stars in relation to the lines, focusing at first on the Pleiades, a cluster of seven stars that, according to 16th-century Spanish chroniclers, ancient Peruvians considered especially portentous. "If the stars rose large and bright," one Spaniard wrote of the cluster, "the crops would ripen well; if they were small, the people expected to suffer."

The task quickly proved onerous, since not only did Reiche have to walk and map the lines, but she also had to perform countless mathematical calculations using only pencil and paper. Her drudgery was compounded by the fact that because of a gradual change in the earth's axis of rotation, the stars seemed to shift in position by about one degree per century. If those who created the lines truly intended for them to align with stars, compensating for their movement would have entailed the periodic redrawing of the geoglyphs, which in itself would go a long way toward explaining the spokelike configuration of many of the lines. For Reiche, however, the additional lines had a more immediate impact: even more walking and yet more calculations.

In the end, Reiche's studies occupied her for decades. Well into the 1980s, when she was in her 80s, Reiche was still on the desert, eager to prove that the Nazca lines were actually sight lines to the stars and that many of the animal shapes represented constellations. Increasingly frail in her later years, she bolstered her waning energy with herbal remedies, drawing from a pharmacopoeia that included bruised alfalfa leaves—to Reiche, the "elixir of youth"—and the occasional jump-start of brown beer, which, she claimed, had once cured her of malaria.

Unfortunately, Reiche's lifetime of hard work counted for little in the minds of other scholars, many of whom seemed to think the ground drawings were unworthy of serious investigation simply because they had captured the public imagination. The Peruvian archaeologist Hans Horkheimer spoke for many in the academic community when in a report published in 1947 he questioned the need for so complicated a calendar, especially if its sole purpose was merely to predict the most propitious time to plant. "Why did the ancients

139

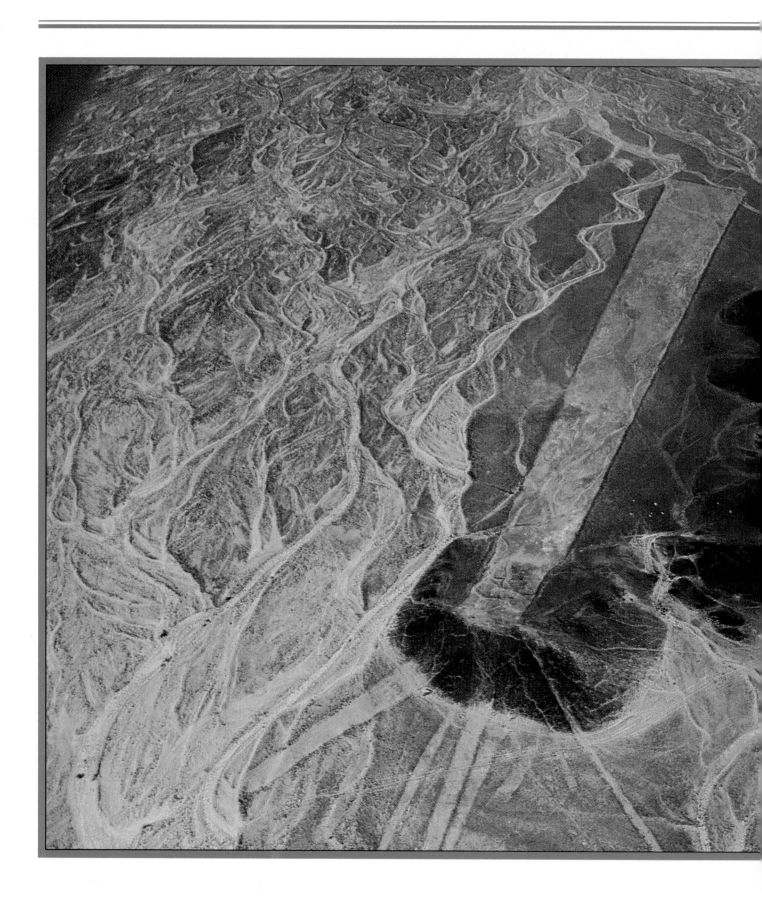

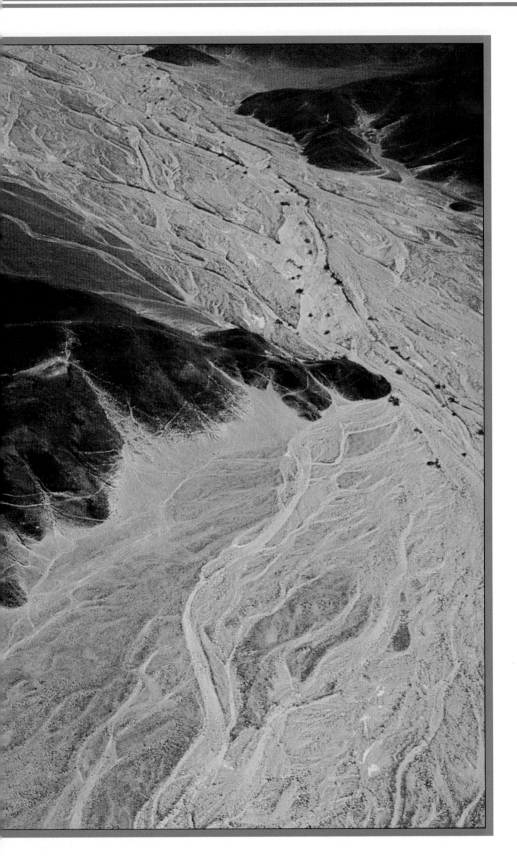

A trapezoid, the most common geometric form among the numerous Nazca ground drawings, or geoglyphs, marks the desert floor of the Pampa de San José near the town of Nazca. According to one theory, such shapes may have been intended to connect symbolically with water sources. They apparently were used as ritual walkways in ceremonies aimed at bringing water to the area.

need lines many kilometers long or clearings a hundred meters wide to mark the position of something in the sky?" asked Horkheimer. Moreover, he wondered, "Why do some of the clearings which supposedly look towards the sun face instead to the south where no heavenly body graces the sky?"

Horkheimer posited a more down-to-earth theory than the one proposed by Reiche. In the same report he suggested that the lines were part of a cult of ancestor worship, at once physically connecting the graves of local clan members to small plazas, where the descendants of the deceased could stage ritual chain dances, and spiritually linking the living to the dead. But while plausible, Horkheimer's theory was undermined by a fundamental flaw, since so far not one grave has ever been found on the pampa.

Other experts joined the growing chorus of criticism. Some suggested that the animal and plant shapes on the pampa had no ritual or symbolic meaning at all, but were simply artistic expressions—preexisting forms that ancient artists liberated from the terrain in much the same way that sculptors are said to free statues from blocks of uncut marble. According to this theory, such giant shapes as the monkey or the hummingbird *(pages 136-137)* were possibly meant to be experienced by walking, not viewing. "Thus one would perceive with the body every sinuous turn in the labyrinthine tail or the delicate curvature of each individual fragment of avian plumage," wrote one scholar. "Like negotiating a curve on a highway, one lives through it from beginning to end."

Still more investigators took Maria Reiche to task for her precalculator, precomputer computations. In 1968 Gerald Hawkins headed a team of scientists and surveyors who mapped the lines on one section of the pampa, then used a computer to sight those lines against the known positions of stars on various dates in the past. The results showed that although a few of the lines may point to the Pleiades and a few others may correspond to the solstice positions of the sun and moon, these "hits" were no more than could be accounted for by mere chance. Hawkins came to the conclusion that while he could not say what the lines were, he knew what they were not. The lines "as a whole cannot be explained as astronomical nor are they calendric," he wrote.

Reiche countered that Hawkins was guilty of inadequate sampling and that his findings were decidedly "unscientific." But the damage was done, and in the future the academic community would continue to give her short shrift. To add insult to injury, in that same year, 1968, the Swiss hotelier-turned-writer Erich von Däniken published a best-selling book in which he claimed that the lines were actually runways for ancient astronauts. In von Däniken's words, the lines were a message from their builders to the circling spacemen. "Land here!" the lines seemed to cry out. "Everything has been prepared as you ordered."

Although von Däniken's theory had no scientific leg to stand on, his book touched off a stampede of visitors to the pampa eager for their own close encounter with the purported runways. "So many people come here now since that spaceman story," Reiche complained in 1976, sensitive as always to the "human erosion" caused by throngs of tourists tramping, trucking, and even ballooning across the vulnerable desert surface for a view of the ground drawings.

Some of the lines appear either to converge on or to radiate from so-called line centers, depending on which theory an observer subscribes to, and to some these configurations have all the appearance of Inca quipus writ large on the landscape. The quipu was an elaborate memory aid—in its day a technological improvement over the old, but not necessarily reliable, string on the finger. Like Braille, it was largely a tactile form of language, and it consisted of a single cord, from which any number of knotted strings were strung. Each string, each knot, a particular knot's position on the string, and even the number of turns in the knot, not to mention the color and twist of the yarn, encoded information—anything from historical events and census data to an accounting of the annual tribute a ruler was due or owed to others. Unfortunately, a quipu could be interpreted only by a *quipu camayoc*, or professional quipu keeper. As a result, surviving quipus pose an all-but-indecipherable riddle to modern-day scholars.

Quipus were, in design if not in intent, hand-held versions of the Inca *ceque* system, an array of imaginary lines that formed sacred pathways radiating in all directions from the heart of the Inca capital, Cuzco, in much the same way that the strings of a quipu radiated from their central cord. The ceques were marked by hundreds of shrines, or huacas, which were strung along individual ceques like the knots of a quipu. These huacas, the Inca believed, were animated by spirits that, if not appeased, could pre-

Portrayals of warriors with wounded knees, as depicted by the Nazca vessel below, are found on but a half-dozen ceramics, the only such representations of casualties in all of Nazca art. Here the victim cradles his slashed knee between his hands. Beneath his eyes and on his cheeks are tatoos. Lines above the lips and on the chin may be meant to suggest facial hair.

cipitate all manner of misery, including drought and famine.

Since different kinship groups were expected to worship at the huacas on different days of the year, the ceque system as a whole functioned as a kind of ritual calendar. But the system appears to have had a number of purposes, encoding such social information as the allocation of land and water rights, among other things. Some scholars, including North American astronomer Anthony Aveni, also believe that several of the Inca huacas located on the horizon served as the endpoints of sight lines, along which various celestial bodies could be observed on important dates during the year, among them the rising and setting of the sun on the solstices and the appearance of the all-important Pleiades.

Not surprisingly, scholars early on were aware of the similarity between the Nazca lines and the Inca ceques and quipus. Indeed, as far back as 1939 Mejía used the word *ceque* to describe the Nazca lines, while Kosok once proposed that the piles of stones located along some of the lines may have recorded numerical, calendrical, and astronomical information, not unlike the knots of a quipu. But it was 1977 before Aveni first realized that the Nazca lines might have more in common with the ceques than their respective linearity, and that the lines, like the ceques, might in fact have had not one, but any number of uses.

Aveni came to Nazca in 1981 at the helm of a team of researchers, each of whom brought different skills to the task of uncovering the purpose and meaning of the lines. Together they would spend the next several years mapping the pampa, piecing together the archaeological record, examining the lines in their cultural context, and probing anew any hidden astronomical implications.

The team's approach to the lines was unusual in that its members were convinced that the geoglyphs had to be walked to be understood. Ironically, with the notable exception of Maria Reiche, few who investigated the lines had ever bothered to walk them. Moreover, even Reiche, like most of the early investigators, never seemed to consider the possibility that since no one theory appeared to explain the lines adequately, perhaps different lines had been constructed for different reasons.

Aveni and his colleagues would eventually conclude that the lines had almost certainly been created to be moved across, although they remained unsure whether that movement entailed walking, running, or ritual dancing. Lacking descriptive texts and representations of the ancients that might shed light on how they used the lines, scholars have turned to studying the traditions of modern Indians. For instance, a 1987 description of participants in Qoyllur Rit'i, the principal modern Andean pilgrimage, suggests that their forebears may have danced along the lines: "Suddenly they arose as a single body and proceeded to file down the hillside at a trot in two columns, flags streaming in the wind. All the musicians were playing the same tune. The two lines of dancers wheeled, wove, and zigzagged across the landscape, successively converging, crossing, and separating in a serpentine choreography."

Aveni also took note of the fact that many of the lines clambered single-mindedly up hills and down gullies, as if, in his words, "ordained to be straight for some overriding ritual reason." He believed that reason was primarily related to the flow of water. In the desert, where water is always a precious commodity, and especially in the delicate ecological transition zone between the coast and the mountains, the lines may have played a part in some ritual intended to sum-

This doll-like Nazca-style figure, just three inches high, was probably created for a burial. The maker formed a body of stiff, multilayered plant stalks wrapped in leafy material and secured by cotton yarn, then covered it with a skin and tunic, both woven separately. The facial features were embroidered, and little fingers and toes were made of heavy yarn. Human hair falls from the head, some of it fashioned into tiny braids tied with cotton threads.

mon water up from its underground reservoirs and down from its mountain sources. Aveni noted in his report that similar rituals are still conducted today on similar pathways elsewhere in the Andes. He further observed that of those lines that could be traced with any certainty, the majority connect points that are somehow related to the flow of water, including the bends in rivers and dunes that overlook rivers. Line centers in particular appeared to have been sited near water sources, and even the axes of trapezoids were found to be frequently oriented in the direction of the flow of water.

All this, however, was not to deny the possibility that the lines might also have had an astronomical connection, as Kosok and Reiche had argued earlier. "Our analysis, if somewhat tedious, reveals that astronomy, though largely lost in the data, may nevertheless be faintly present," the Aveni team admitted. "Though there are no obvious clustering tendencies that can be directly attributed to astronomical factors, sky phenomena that were recognized and that possessed meaning in the coastal environment seem to turn up in the alignments." And one of the most prominent, the study revealed, occurs on the day in late October when the sun makes its way across the zenith—a time that just happens to coincide with the expected return of water to the otherwise dry streambeds.

In the course of their research the Aveni team also proved that the Nazca ground drawings may not have been the labor-intensive feats of engineering alluded to by the British ethnographer and archaeologist Geoffrey Bushnell, who once attributed the lines to a "great deal of skill and not a little disciplined labor." To the contrary, Aveni and only a dozen volunteers in 1984 created what he called a "home-made Nazca line"—a rectangular strip about 15 times as long as it was wide that was aligned on a distant mountain peak and ended in a loosely coiled spiral. Two workers holding upright sticks successfully oriented the geoglyph, and pieces of string were used to measure the radii of the three arcs that formed the spiral.

Then the group broke into two squads, one of which cleared the area within the figure, leaving small piles of stones that the other volunteers used to darken the borders of the geoglyph, which covered an area of about 37 square yards. Completed in 90 minutes, the exercise, Aveni wrote, showed "that neither a complex technology nor a sophisticated knowledge of classical geometry detailed through a 'blueprint' is required to construct such a figure. Moreover, the amount of labor is surprisingly small."

Based on the results of his trial, the archaeologist concluded that 100 persons working 10 hours a day could have cleared an area the size of a good-sized trapezoid, or about 2,400 square yards, in as little as two days. "Indeed, given a work force of 10,000 (and inspired by a sound work ethic), all the features on the pampa could have been constructed in a matter of a few years," Aveni asserted.

The German archaeologist Max Uhle, one of the first scholars to document the many Andean civilizations that thrived long before that of the Incas, once numbered the Nazca among his "protean" cultures. In its earliest phase it was most likely contemporary with the Paracas Necrópolis tradition. Settling in river valleys, the Nazca people established small villages of adobe buildings and wattle-and-daub homes. There, judging from the dating of their bountiful ceramics, they would endure as a culture for some 700 years, until they were first absorbed by the expanding Wari empire in the sixth century AD and later engulfed by the Inca. Any remnants of Nazca culture that managed to survive were all but obliterated in the cross fire of a

Ocean creatures are frequently portrayed in Nazca art, as in the geoglyph and ceramic vessel below, both representing a killer whale. The vessel portrays the animal with human arms, while the ground drawing shows it clutching a human trophy head. As the most powerful mammal of their marine environment, the whale obviously impressed the Nazca, who may well have incorporated it into their fertility rites.

16th-century civil war fought between opposing camps of Spaniards.

Before then, however, Nazca potters would turn out especially fine polychrome ceramics whose design and technical virtuosity eclipsed even that of Paracas. Some surviving examples, effigies made to resemble humans and animals, echo the designs of many of the ground drawings *(pages 146-147)*. In fact, this association of the pottery with the ground drawings was a critical step that allowed archaeologists to attribute them to the Nazca. This conclusion was corroborated by the discovery of similar, broken pottery on the Pampa Colorada itself, although archaeologists are quick to point out that such sherds may indicate not who made the ground drawings, but only who walked upon or otherwise used them.

In vivid contrast to the monochrome Necrópolis ceramics, Nazca pottery is distinguished by as many as 11 colors on a single vessel and by its frequent depiction of human trophy heads, an indication to some scholars of a distinctly belligerent society. Even more telling, a number of actual heads have been recovered at Nazca sites. Trophy heads were also a motif in Nazca textiles, which had their roots in the Paracas tradition but, unlike the Nazca ceramics, never exceeded their Paracas counterparts in artistry.

Since both the pottery and the textiles were included in graves, both may have been created specifically as funerary offerings. Nazca cemeteries, like those of Paracas, suffered grievously at the hands of the huaqueros. But as in Paracas burial sites, flexed bodies were found wrapped in textiles and surrounded by pottery and other grave offerings. These goods sometimes included hammered gold, making the graves all the more attractive to the looters.

Nazca technology was limited in scope and is best exemplified by the construction of subsurface water conduits, an innovation that underscores the importance of water in the lives of this desert farming culture. These stone-lined channels, called *pukios*, were designed to tap subterranean, year-round supplies of water. Once on the surface, the water was stored in reservoirs, and these, in turn, fed a network of irrigation canals. Individual pukios sometimes stretch more than 500 yards.

Water may also have figured in the location of the sprawling Nazca ceremonial center at Cahuachi. Indeed, this largest of all known Nazca sites occupies not only one bank of the Nazca River, but also a spot where several springs lie. These flow even when the river does not, and they supposedly had their source in an aquifer fed

This head most likely belonged to a prisoner taken in combat by Nazca warriors, who used such trophies in religious rites intended to ensure crop fertility. The head was cut from the body, the brain removed and replaced by cotton cloth or vegetable matter, and a rope attached through a hole in the forehead. One scholar, basing his theory on ethnographic evidence, suggests that the lips were pinned shut with huarango *thorns to keep the victim's avenging spirit from harming the killer.*

by waters from Cerro Blanco, Nazca's sacred mountain. Accordingly, Cahuachi may have been perceived by the ancient inhabitants of the area as a magical place and a natural huaca in its own right.

Beginning early in the first century AD and continuing over the course of the next 750 years or so, the site became the location of more than 40 mounds of different sizes that were separated by forecourts and plazas. Each mound was created by building upon or enclosing a hill in an adobe facade, allowing the builders to achieve the maximum effect with minimum effort. Largest of all was the so-called Great Temple, a stepped pyramid some 60 feet high.

Despite the claims of earlier investigators that Cahuachi had been the seat of a Nazca empire, research conducted in the 1980s by Helaine Silverman suggested that the site may not have been a place of permanent habitation, but a center of pilgrimage that was used on a frequent, though intermittent, basis. More important, Silverman argued that the ground drawings lying on the Pampa de Atarco, immediately to the south of Cahuachi, were once part of the same religious phenomenon.

Not only do some of these lines point to major mounds at Cahuachi, but certain mounds within the ceremonial center provide an excellent view of the line- and figure-bedecked Pampa de Nazca, which sprawls across the Nazca River to the north. Silverman suggested that the lines served two functions, the first of which had to do with what she described as transforming natural terrain into cultural terrain. "To draw a wall around an area is to bring it within one's sphere of control," she explained. "At Cahuachi, where the artificial mounds are not much different from the unmodified natural hills around them, this 'bringing within' was a necessary cultural act to create social space. Likewise, the tracing of the lines on the empty pampa surface brought this space within the human sphere."

The lines' second function, Silverman argued, was to serve as sacred roads that not only carried ritually dressed and masked pilgrims to the ceremonial center but, during the course of their journey, changed them as well. Dancing along the pathways, she wrote, human beings entered into a phase "that transformed them from the ordinary people they were to the ritual social beings they would become when they arrived at Cahuachi."

At least some of the ceremonies they participated in there, she speculates, had to have the purpose of predicting and ensuring an adequate supply of precious water, which was a source of urgent concern to the entire Nazca region. Only such rites having to do with agricultural fertility could have motivated so many people to make the pilgrimage.

In all likelihood, the timing of such pilgrimages and ceremonies would have been governed by a ritual calendar, and that calendar, writes Silverman, is etched onto the pampa. Silverman echoes Aveni in comparing the Nazca lines to the Inca's multifunctional ceques, arguing that among their many uses the Nazca lines served as both a ritual and an astronomical calendar. Moreover, the lines may have been related to water sources and possibly associated with kinship groups and the division of land and water rights. As for the line centers, Silverman theorizes that they may have been places of convergence and the scenes of religious or sacrificial ceremonies.

Even after Cahuachi fell into decline, it continued to function as a mortuary center and as a place of votive offerings. Nevertheless, what had once been so sacred would in time be profaned, since the fate of Cahuachi, like the fate of so many other sites in Nazca and Paracas, would eventually rest in the hands of the huaqueros.

For the archaeologist, for whom the search for El Dorado continues, such desecration compounds the difficulty of reconstructing Peru's lost civilizations. Yet, as the work of Helaine Silverman so eloquently attests, scholars have wrested from the desert some of its long-held secrets and pieced together at least part of the puzzle of the Peruvian past. Indeed, there is comfort to be found in the guarded optimism of Maria Reiche, who, in writing about her own quest to fathom the meaning of the Nazca lines, wrote what could be the watchword of searchers everywhere. "One day we expect to decipher the puzzle," she declared in one breath, before acknowledging a hint of doubt in the next, "if God so wishes."

THE PERPLEXING SHROUDS

Through its vibrant and colorful textiles, the Paracas culture of Peru has left behind a rich legacy that teases with its elusiveness. Rife with symbols that have lost their meaning in the absence of a guide, the textiles can seem to defy interpretation. Yet the specialists studying them have managed to glean clues from the embroidered images that provide insights into the lives and minds of individuals who between 450 and 175 BC went to their graves wrapped in yards and yards of the cloth. As the following pages indicate, the textiles' lively images suggest an imaginative intimacy with the forces of nature—and seemingly with the forces of the supernatural as well.

Still, as North American archaeologist Ann H. Peters says, "Looking at these textiles, we will always have more questions than answers." No one knows, for instance, what kind of social role the men in the detail above from a 2,000-year-old grave wrapping play as they squarely face the viewer. They hold a staff in one hand and a severed trophy head in the other. Some scholars say such "warrior figures" may represent the leaders of distinct lineages, but other experts believe the owner of this particular textile would have been a warrior who used the design to proclaim his role in the community. Peters takes a larger view and suggests the figures stand for human predatory power.

The societies that placed value in such wrappings would have had to call upon the services of a small army of specialists to produce them: cotton farmers, gatherers of wild vicuna wool, herders of llamas and alpacas, and dyers, weavers, and of course the embroiderers, whose brilliant work has survived for millennia under the dry conditions of Peru's Paracas Peninsula. But whatever ancient secrets these textiles may keep, at least one message is clear: The exquisite burial wrappings served as a costly indication of status, for only the bodies of older males were found bundled in multiple layers of the most magnificent fabrics.

TIMELESS DANCE OF THE ANIMALS

Hundreds of the intricately embroidered textiles testify to a close relationship between their owners and the physical world. Birds are most prevalent among the beasts illustrated, but there are wildcats, too, and strange hybrid zoomorphs that combine feline characteristics with those of other animals. Snakelike creatures, fish, monkeys, rodents, and lizards also appear, as do llamas. Even more numerous than animals are images of humans costumed as animals or, in some cases, as vegetation—perhaps participants in some sort of eclectic rituals. Such impersonators may have hoped to take on the qualities of the living things they represented.

The creators of the images apparently had a spiritual relationship with nature, as the Inca people would a thousand years later and as some Andeans still do. For festive occasions, Incas would wear zoomorphic costumes with designs that recall the scenes in the embroideries. Handwoven textiles continue to be important in the region today. The people of Coroma, Bolivia, for example, take out their precious heirloom weavings and use them in rituals designed to placate their ancestors' spirits and the forces of nature.

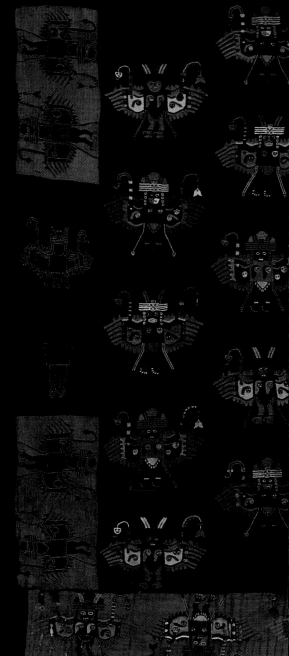

Embroidered on a skirt, the pampas cat above is shown with a flowering lima bean stem that has pods attached. Since it was often depicted with cultivated crops, some think that the small but powerful predator may have been seen as a guardian of the earth and that its embroidered image was the badge of an earth cult. At right, from a mantle, or cloak, is a human wearing a pampas cat impersonator's costume.

A host of five-inch-high embroidered bird impersonators, carrying trophy heads and snake-headed batons, cover the mantle above. Because no actual impersonator costumes have been found in the graves, despite the many detailed embroidered images of people wearing them in the weavings, North American art historian Anne Paul thinks community leaders must have passed on their impersonator roles and apparel to successors at death.

The dancer at right wears a shark costume—or perhaps a hybrid shark-falcon costume, because the fins display the black-and-white zigzag pattern traditionally used to convey falcon feathers. As a major predator in the ocean's food chain, the shark may have been viewed as the guardian of the genera-tive sea, perhaps even as a metaphor for it.

Called the Ecstatic Shaman, this grinning figure with arched body may well be flying—at least metaphorically. One hand holds a feathered fan that sug-gests the power and attributes of a bird, an animal revered in some cultures as the patron of enlightening intoxica-tion. The other hand grasps a baton or a tube for inhaling hallucinogens. The pectoral on the torso could be a magic mirror that would have been seen as imparting special vision to the shaman,

For the people of Paracas—who knew well their own myths and symbols, mystical beliefs and religious rituals, and accounts of rulers, victories, and defeats—the embroidered textiles overflowed with meaning.

Scholars can go only on what they see represented in the designs. Through careful research they have identified many of the specific animals and plants in the images, for instance, allowing interpretations based on their place in the local landscape, mountains, and irrigated desert bordered by ocean. Theories rarely win general agreement, however. Some scholars think bean images are ideograms in a lost writing system, others that beans are symbols for trophy heads. Beans may also have been used, like stones, in divination rites, perhaps to determine the best times to plant crops.

Probably the most impenetrable designs are those from the last period of Paracas culture, such as the two presented here. They may never be interpreted fully; but even if they are not, their beauty will continue to remind viewers of the enduring genius of the Paracas weavers.

On the mantle above, a figure who could be a supernatural or mythological being brims with perplexing detail. The face appears to be human, while the feet seem distinctly monkeylike. Appendages, or streamers, loaded with symbols, issue from various points, their meanings hidden.

Seen in a closeup, the being at right has human hands and feet and wears a cat-skin headdress with bean spots. A wide streamer sprouting from his mouth bears shaman images along its length and culminates in a bird figure recognized as a South American species, the whiskered banded nightjar.

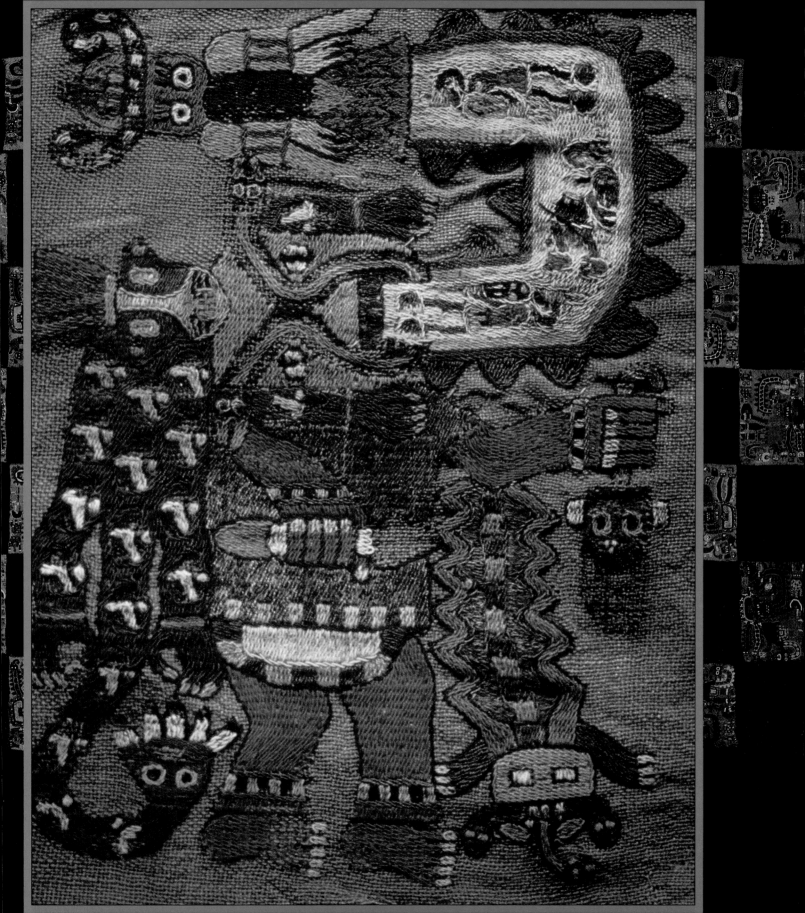

A CHAIN OF CULTURES IN THE NEW WORLD

Artisans in Peru's southern Andes had probably begun working gold, found in streambeds, as early as 1500 BC. Knowledge of their metallurgical techniques spread over the centuries to the north and central coasts, the northern Andes, the Panamanian isthmus, and farther north. There, the peoples described at right—almost certainly descendants of immigrants who walked across the land bridge that connected Asia and North America at least 12,000 years ago—developed their goldworking skills to heights of technical and artistic mastery.

By the time the conquistadors landed in South America in the early 16th century AD, numerous New World cultures had already flourished and died out, vanquished by natural disasters or by neighboring peoples. The Europeans entered a realm that lay between two great empires—Aztec Mexico and Inca Peru—and found smaller, simpler societies, the domains of local chieftains. Like all New World cultures, these peoples did not use the wheel and did not work in iron—two developments that had already transformed life in the Old World. But they had created societies organized around massive stone monuments and a settled way of life with abundant food, affording them the luxury of an inventive and productive artist class.

CENTRAL AMERICA
AD 500-1502

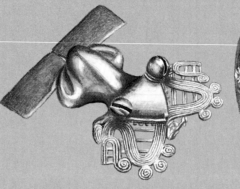

CAST-GOLD FROG

Toward AD 500, as villages in the area known today as Costa Rica and Panama became consolidated into a few dozen small chiefdoms, cultures made up of agricultural villages gave way to more complex societies. The people cleared forests with stone axes, developed an ornate style of hand-built (not wheel-thrown) pottery, and learned the goldworking arts. The Diquís, on the southwest coast, found rich sources of gold along riverbanks, and their smiths made exuberant effigies of wildlife, such as the cast-gold frog above, with its bulbous, protruding eyes and its mouth holding two fanciful, ornate serpents. (The stylized, flattened feet are seen on some human figures as well.) Diquís artists sought to capture the divine life force by making images of animals that embodied it. Costa Rica, whose name is Spanish for Rich Coast, was so named from conquistadors' glowing accounts of local chiefs in their golden regalia.

The Coclé in Panama were another highly skilled goldworking people. At Sitio Conte, a Coclé burial site used between AD 500 and 700, archaeologists have unearthed grave goods ranging from sparse to splendid, showing a stratified society in which the chiefs' graves were especially opulent. A chieftain of Darien, in Panama, told the Spaniards his golden ornaments came "from the sky"—before admitting to their earthbound source.

NORTHERN ANDES
4000 BC-AD 1600

CALIMA BREASTPLATE

What is now Colombia and Ecuador once hosted a variety of pre-Columbian cultures. The Quimbaya and the Tolima, for instance, lived in parallel valleys separated by mountains. The Muisca had their mountain range, the Sinú the marshes and lagoons of the northern coastal plain, and the Tairona the mountains near the coast. Each group lived in wood houses with stone foundations in towns organized into loose states headed by chieftains, and all were goldworkers.

Here the Spaniards came upon not only the legend of El Dorado, among the Muisca, but one of their first hoards of New World gold as well. A letter by the explorer Vasco Núñez de Balboa in 1513 reported a lively gold trade among the indigenous peoples. Twenty years later, a Spanish expedition to the Sinú "opened rich graves" that yielded for the king's treasury "about 110 lbs. of fine gold and 53 lbs. of base [alloyed] gold"—and the rush was on. Of the Sinú work that survives in museums, some is false filigree—cast gold that looks as if made of fine wires.

Though the Sinú dated back an estimated thousand years or so, they were preceded, in the mountain valleys to the south, by the Calima, who had learned goldworking techniques some 500 years earlier. The Calima created hammered and repoussé, or embossed, works like the breastplate above as ornaments for their royalty, but they had already disappeared before the conquistadors arrived.

ANDES: NORTH AND CENTRAL COASTS 10,000 BC-AD 1476

MOCHE EARSPOOL

In the river valleys of Peru's dry coastal plain, evidence of human habitation goes back almost 12,000 years. Stone foundations in the highlands are the oldest monumental ruins in the New World; roughly contemporary with Egypt's first pyramids, they were built in 3000 BC. Inhabitants along the coast constructed religious centers with massive platforms of stone and adobe and wove the figures of humans and animals into their textiles. Shortly after 2000 BC, pottery making and gold and copper metallurgy developed.

The Moche, one of the greatest pre-Inca civilizations, arose in the Moche Valley about AD 100 and extended their dominion along more than 340 miles of coast. Builders of sophisticated irrigation channels to sustain their crops in the rainless valleys, they also constructed solid adobe pyramids—including South America's largest, the Pyramid of the Sun, near Trujillo. In these they buried their lords with such exquisite gifts as bowls, necklaces, nose ornaments, and earspools *(above)* made of gold, silver, and gilded copper and inlaid with shell and precious stones.

For reasons that are unclear, the Moche disappeared sometime before AD 800. They were succeeded by the Lambayeque and Sicán cultures, which competed for dominance for about 50 years. The Chimu emerged victorious around 1375, forming an empire that eventually embraced a longer stretch of coastline than the Moche, but they gave way to the Inca in 1476.

ANDES: SOUTH COAST 4500 BC-AD 600

NAZCA PAINTED DISH

Nomadic hunters roamed the southern Andes before 4500 BC, but as hunting gave way to fishing and farming, coastal settlements arose. As early as 1800 BC, some river mouths became the sites of ceremonial centers, U-shaped complexes with impressive stone and adobe platforms. Lacking ceramics and metals, artists carved designs on gourds or wove them into textiles.

On a wind-swept peninsula far to the south of the Moche lands, the Paracas culture held sway for almost 800 years, from 600 BC to AD 175. Goldsmiths made ornaments that were buried with the dead, but they apparently confined themselves to the hammering technique and never produced work of the refinement found among metalworkers to the north, in present-day Colombia. Paracas weavers achieved great artistry, however, embellishing woolen garments with embroidered designs worked in dyed or natural fiber. The textiles are thought to have identified the elite of the culture, who likely wore them on ceremonial occasions.

The Nazca culture, which flourished from 100 BC to AD 600, descended from the Paracas. Nazca textiles and ceramics were technically and artistically masterful. On the painted plate above, the three heads with tongues out and dangling paws represent a feline from their mythology. The Nazca also built pyramidal structures for religious rites, but they are best known for their desert-floor drawings, the Nazca lines, whose purpose is under debate.

ANDES: HIGHLAND REGION 1400 BC-AD 1100

CHAVIN FELINE DEITY

Between 1400 and 300 BC, the Andean highlands nurtured the Chavin culture, which archaeologists have named after Chavin de Huantar, an imposing ceremonial center located near present-day Huaraz. An enterprising people, the Chavin united many earlier traditions, borrowing the complex's U-shaped plan from coastal residents and adopting images of animals from forest dwellers along the Amazon. Scholars believe the site was the focal point of a powerful new religion centered on an oracle said to reside there.

Advances in metalworking and weaving attributed to the Chavin may have been undertaken in the service of the new cult, as portable religious objects in gold and textiles helped to spread the faith. Chavin goldsmiths used hammering, repoussé, soldering, and welding to make objects like the four-and-a-half-inch ornament above, probably once sewn to a priest's vestment. It shows the snarling jaguar, a symbol of supernatural power prevalent in Chavin culture and in later Peruvian art. By the time the Chavin style died out, the metalsmiths had passed on their techniques—and their gods—to other Peruvian peoples, including the Moche.

Next to emerge were the Tiahuanaco and the Wari, two influential cultures that scholars consider the first truly imperial states in the Andes. Between 300 BC and AD 1100, they dominated the region and helped lay the groundwork for later Inca rule.

ACKNOWLEDGMENTS

The editors wish to thank the following individuals and institutions for their valuable assistance in the preparation of this volume:

Walter Alva, Museo Brüning, Lambayeque, Peru; Ferdinand Anton, Munich; Sumru Aricanli, American Museum of Natural History, New York; Warwick Bray, London; Richard L. Burger, Yale University, New Haven; Anita Cook, The Catholic University of America, Washington, D.C.; Christian Eckmann, Römisch-Germanischen Zentralmuseum, Mainz; Benjamin Guerrero, Museo Nacional de Antropología y Arqueología, Lima, Peru; Sonia Guillen, Fundación de Bioantropología, Lima, Peru; Pamela Hearne, University of Pennsylvania, Philadelphia; William Isbell, State University New York, Binghamton; Donna McClelland, San Marino, Calif.; Phyllis Pitluga, Adler Planetarium, Chicago; Donald A. Proulx, University of Massachusetts, Amherst; Johan Reinhard, Woodlands Mountain Institute, Franklin, West Virginia; Helaine Silverman, University of Illinois, Urbana-Champaign; Richard F. Townsend, The Art Institute of Chicago, Chicago; Friedrich-Wilhelm von Hase, Römisch-Germanischen Zentralmuseum, Mainz; Margaret Young, The Cleveland Museum of Art, Cleveland.

PICTURE CREDITS

BIBLIOGRAPHY

BOOKS

Alva, Walter, and Christopher Donnan. *Royal Tombs of Sipán*. Los Angeles: Regents of the University of California, 1993.

Alva, Walter, Maiken Fecht, Peter Schauer, and Michael Tellenbach. *Das Fürstengrab von Sipán*. Mainz: Verlag des Römisch-Germanischen Zentralmuseums, 1989.

Anton, Ferdinand:
Ancient Peruvian Textiles. London: Thames and Hudson, 1987.
The Art of Ancient Peru. New York: G. P. Putnam's, 1972.

Aveni, Anthony (ed.). *The Lines of Nazca*. Philadelphia: American Philosophical Society, 1990.

Bankes, George:
Moche Pottery from Peru. London: British Museum Publications, 1980.
Peruvian Pottery. Aylesbury, England: Shire Publications, 1989.

Benson, Elizabeth P. *The Mochica: A Culture of Peru*. London: Thames and Hudson, 1972.

Benson, Elizabeth P. (ed.). *Death and the Afterlife in Pre-Columbian America*. Washington, D.C.: Dumbarton Oaks Research Library and Collections, Trustees for Harvard University, 1975.

Bray, Warwick. *The Gold of El Dorado*. London: Times Newspapers, 1978.

Bray, Warwick, and Andrea Brezzi. *La Terra Dell' El Dorado*. Milan: Fondazione Milano, 1991.

Brettell, Richard. *The Museum of the Americas*. London: Apollo Magazine, 1993.

Burger, Richard L. *Chavin and the Origins of Andean Civilization*. London: Thames and Hudson, 1992.

Chapman, Walker. *The Search for El Dorado*. Indianapolis: Bobbs-Merrill, 1967.

Cordy-Collins, Alana, and Jean Stern. *Pre-Columbian Art History: Selected Readings*. Palo Alto: Peek Publications, 1977.

Daggett, Richard E. "Discovery and Controversy." In *Paracas: Art and Architecture*, edited by Anne Paul. Iowa City: University of Iowa Press, 1991.

Dickey, Thomas, John Man, and Henry Wiencek. *The Kings of El Dorado*. Alexandria: Stonehenge Press, 1982.

Donnan, Christopher B.:
Ceramics of Ancient Peru. Los Angeles: Regents of the University of California, 1992.
Moche Art of Peru. Los Angeles: Museum of Cultural History, University of California, 1978.

Donnan, Christopher B. (ed.). *Early Ceremonial Architecture in the Andes*. Washington, D.C.: Dumbarton Oaks Research Library and Collections, Trustees for Harvard University, 1985.

Enslow, Sam. *The Art of Prehispanic Colombia: An Illustrated Cultural and Historical Survey*. Jefferson, N.C.: McFarland, 1990.

Fagan, Brian M. *Kingdoms of Gold, Kingdoms of Jade: The Americas before Columbus*. London: Thames and Hudson, 1991.

Fawcett, P. H. *Exploration Fawcett*. London: Century, 1988.

Furst, Peter T. (ed.). *Flesh of the Gods: The Ritual Use of Hallucinogens*. New York: Praeger, 1972.

Gardner, Joseph L. (ed.). *Mysteries of the Ancient Americas*. Pleasantville, N.Y.: Reader's Digest Association, 1986.

Hadingham, Evan. *Lines to the Mountain Gods: Nazca and the Mysteries of Peru*. New York: Random House, 1987.

Hanson, Earl Parker (ed.). *South from the Spanish Main*. New York: Delacorte Press, 1967.

Hearne, Pamela, and Robert J. Sharer (eds.). *River of Gold: Precolumbian Treasures from Sitio Conte*. Philadelphia: University of Pennsylvania, 1992.

Hemming, John. *The Search for El Dorado*. New York: E. P. Dutton, 1978.

Hidalgo, Francisco. *Oro del Peru*. Text by Aurelio Miro Quesada S. Lima: Editions Delroisse, 1981.

Hoyle, Rafael Larco. *Peru*. Translated by James Hogarth. Geneva: Nagel, 1966.

Johnson, Lucille Lewis (ed.). *Paleoshorelines and Prehistory: An Investigation of Method*. Boca Raton: CRC Press, 1992.

Jones, Julie (ed.). *The Art of Precolumbian Gold: The Jan Mitchell Collection*. Boston: Little, Brown, 1985.

Keatinge, Richard W. (ed.). *Peruvian*

Prehistory: An Overview of Pre-Inca and Inca Society. Cambridge: Cambridge University Press, 1988.

Kolata, Alan. *The Tiwanaku: Portrait of an Andean Civilization*. Cambridge: Blackwell, 1993.

Kosok, Paul. *Life, Land and Water in Ancient Peru*. New York: Long Island University Press, 1965.

Kubler, George. *The Art and Architecture of Ancient America*. Harmondsworth, Middlesex, England: Penguin Books, 1983.

Lapiner, Alan. *Pre-Columbian Art of South America*. New York: Harry N. Abrams, 1976.

Lavalle, José Antonio de, and Werner Lang. *Arte y Tesoros del Perú*. Lima, Peru: Banco de Crédito del Perú en la Cultura, 1981.

Levenson, Jay A. (ed.). *Art in the Age of Exploration: Circa 1492*. Washington, D.C.: National Gallery of Art, 1991.

Lumbreras, Luis G. *The Peoples and Cultures of Ancient Peru*. Translated by Betty J. Meggers. Washington, D.C.: Smithsonian Institution Press, 1974.

Lumbreras, Luis G., Chacho González, and Bernard Lietaer. *Acerca de la Función del Sistema Hidráulico de Chavín*. Lima, Peru: Museo Nacional de Antropología y Arqueología, 1976.

McIntosh, Jane. *The Practical Archaeologist: How We Know What We Know about the Past*. New York: Facts On File Publications, 1986.

Morris, Craig, and Adriana Von Hagen. *The Inka Empire and Its Andean Origins*. New York: Abbeville Press, 1994.

Morrison, Tony:
The Mystery of the Nasca Lines. Suffolk, England: Nonesuch Expeditions, 1987.
Pathways to the Gods. Incorporating the work of Gerald S. Hawkins. New York: Harper & Row, 1978.

Moseley, Michael E. *The Incas and Their Ancestors*. London: Thames and Hudson, 1992.

Moseley, Michael E., David Wagner, and James B. Richardson. "Space Shuttle Imagery of Recent Catastrophic Change along the Arid Andean Coast." In *Paleoshorelines and Prehistory: An Investigation of*

Method, edited by Lucille Lewis Johnson. Boca Raton: CRC Press, 1992.

Naipaul, V. S. *The Loss of El Dorado: A History*. New York: Alfred A. Knopf, 1970.

National Geographic Society. *Peoples and Places of the Past*. Washington, D.C., 1983.

Osborne, Harold. *South American Mythology*. London: Hamlyn, 1968.

Paul, Anne:
  Paracas Ritual Attire: Symbols of Authority in Ancient Peru. Norman: University of Oklahoma Press, 1990.
  "Procedures, Patterns, and Deviations in Paracas Embroidered Textiles: Traces of the Creative Process." In *To Weave for the Sun: Andean Textiles in the Museum of Fine Arts, Boston*, by Rebecca Stone-Miller. Boston: Museum of Fine Arts, 1992.

Paul, Anne (ed.). *Paracas: Art and Architecture*. Iowa City: University of Iowa Press, 1991.

Proulx, Donald A. "The Nasca Style." In *Art of the Andes: Pre-Columbian Sculptured and Painted Ceramics from the Arthur M. Sackler Collections*. Washington, D.C.: Arthur M. Sackler Foundation and the AMS Foundation for the Arts, Sciences and Humanities, 1983.

Raleigh, Sir Walter. *The Discovery of the Large, Rich, and Beautiful Empire of Guiana*. Edited by Robert H. Schomburgk. London: Hakluyt Society, 1596.

Reichel-Dolmatoff, Gerardo:
  Colombia (Ancient Peoples and Places series). New York: Frederick A. Praeger, 1965.
  Goldwork and Shamanism: An Iconographic Study of the Gold Museum. Colombia: Banco de la Republica, 1988.
  The Shaman and the Jaguar. Philadelphia: Temple University Press, 1975.
  Shamanism and Art of the Eastern Tukanoan Indians. New York: E. J. Brill, 1987.

Reinhard, Johan. *The Nazca Lines: A New Perspective on their Origin and Meaning*. Lima: Editorial Los Pinos E.I.R.I., 1986.

Roden, Hans. *Treasure-Seekers*. Translated by Frances Hogarth-Gaute. New York: Walker, 1963.

Rowe, John Howland, and Dorothy Menzel. *Peruvian Archaeology: Selected Readings*. Palo Alto: Peek Publications, 1967.

Sauer, Carl Ortwin. *The Early Spanish Main*. Berkeley: University of California Press, 1969.

Silverman, Helaine. *Cahuachi in the Ancient Nasca World*. Iowa City: University of Iowa Press, 1993.

Tello, Julio C. *Paracas: Primera Parte*. New York: Institute of Andean Research, 1959.

Townsend, Richard F. (ed.). *The Ancient Americas: Art from Sacred Landscapes*. Chicago: The Art Institute of Chicago, 1992.

Von Däniken, Erich. *Chariots of the Gods?: Unsolved Mysteries of the Past*. Translated by Michael Heron. New York: G. P. Putnam's, 1969.

Von Hagen, Victor W. *The Golden Man*. London: Book Club Associates, 1974.

Westwood, Jennifer (ed.). *The Atlas of Mysterious Places*. New York: Weidenfeld & Nicolson, 1987.

Zahm, J. A. *The Quest of El Dorado: The Most Romantic Episode in the History of South American Conquest*. New York: D. Appleton, 1917.

PERIODICALS

Alva, Walter:
  "Richest Unlooted Tomb of a Moche Lord." *National Geographic*, October 1988.
  "Splendors of the Moche: New Royal Tomb Unearthed." *National Geographic*, June 1990.

Carlson, John B. "America's Ancient Skywatchers." *National Geographic*, March 1990.

Donnan, Christopher B.:
  "Masterworks Reveal a Pre-Inca World." *National Geographic*, June 1990.
  "A Precolumbian Smelter from Northern Peru." *Archaeology*, October 1973.

Donnan, Christopher B., and Luis Jaime Castillo. "Finding the Tomb of a Moche Priestess." *Archaeology*, November/December 1992.

Gomez, Linda. "*Life* Visits the Lady of the Lines." *Life Magazine*, November 1984.

Horié, Donna M. "A Family of Nasca Figures." *The Textile Museum Journal*, 1991.

Mason, J. Alden. "Gold from the Grave." *Scientific American*, November 1941.

Moseley, Michael E., and James B. Richardson. "Doomed by Natural Disaster." *Archaeology*, November/December 1992.

Paul, Anne, and Solveig A. Turpin. "The Ecstatic Shaman Theme of Paracas Textiles." *Archaeology*, September/October 1986.

Proulx, Donald A.:
  "Headhunting in Ancient Peru." *Archaeology*, January 1971.
  "Nasca Trophy Heads: Victims of Warfare or Ritual Sacrifice?" *Cultures in Conflict: Current Archaeological Perspectives*, 1989.

Rowe, Ann Pollard. "Nasca Figurines and Costume." *The Textile Museum Journal*, 1991.

Sawyer, Alan R. "Paracas Necropolis Headdress and Face Ornaments." *The Textile Museum*, May 1960.

Schuster, Angela M. H. "Inside the Royal Tombs of the Moche." *Archaeology*, November/December 1992.

Silverman, Helaine. "Beyond the Pampa: The Geoglyphs in the Valleys of Nazca." *National Geographic Research*, 1990.

Toufexis, Anastasia. "The Mummy's Tale." *Time*, March 26, 1994.

Vepřek, S., Ch. Eckmann, J. Th. Elmer. "Recent Progress in the Restoration of Archeological Metallic Artifacts by Means of Low-Pressure Plasma Treatment." *Plasma Chemistry and Plasma Processing*, Vol. 8, No. 4, 1988.

Vepřek, S., J. Th. Elmer, Ch. Eckmann, and Jurčik-Rajman. "Restoration and Conservation of Archeological Artifacts by Means of a New Plasma-Chemical Method." *Journal of the Electrochemical Society*, Vol. 134, No. 10, October 1987.

Vreeland, James M. "Day of the Dead." *Archaeology*, November/December 1992.

Wilford, John Noble. "Tuberculosis Found to Be Old Disease in New World." *New York Times*, March 15, 1994.

OTHER SOURCES

Alva, Walter, and Christopher Donnan. Interview by Ina Jaffe. *Morning Edition*. National Public Radio, Sepember 22, 1993.

"Conference on Chavín." Washington, D.C.: Dumbarton Oaks, October 1968.

Donnan, Christopher. Interview by Jacqueline Deslauriers. *Weekend Edition*. KCRW radio, October 17, 1993.

"El Dorado: The Gold of Ancient Colombia." Exhibition catalog. Center for Inter-American Relations and The American Federation of Arts, New York, 1974.

McClelland, Donna. "Reproducing Moche Fineline Drawings." Unpublished paper. San Marino, Calif.: University of California at Los Angeles, 1994.

McEwan, Gordon. "An Introduction to Andean Art and Archaeology." Unpublished manuscript in possession of author, 1990.

"Sweat of the Sun, Tears of the Moon: Gold and Emerald Treasures of Colombia." Exhibition catalog. Natural History Museum Alliance, Los Angeles, 1981.

INDEX

N

PACIFIC OCEAN

CARIBBEAN SEA

Panama

Colombia

Ecuador

Peru

PACIFIC OCEAN

ATLANTIC OCEAN

MUISCA GOLD OFFERING PIECE